Sanskrit and Manipuri

Dr. A. Sudha Devi

RAJESH PUBLICATIONS
NEW DELHI - 110 002

ISBN : 978-93-83684-00-7 (H.B.)
ISBN : 978-93-83684-01-4 (P.B.)

Published by:
Sanjay Gupta
Rajesh Publications
1, Ansari Road, Darya Ganj,
New Delhi - 110 002

Typesetting by:
Ritu Pandey
New Delhi - 110 002

First Published in India 2014

Printed in India at:
Vijeta Offset Press
Delhi - 110002

Price : **Rs. 500.00** (H.B.)
Price : **Rs. 200.00** (P.B.)

In Loving Memory

of

My Father

Ram Prasad Gupta

and

Parents-in-Law

Akoijam Pujari Devi

&

Akoijam Babuchand Singh

who were great source of inspiration

in my Life

Preface

This book is an approach of comparative study of two languages belonging to entirely two different language groups and it presents a new horizon for study.

I have divided my book in eight chapters. First chapter Introduction provides an outline of the subject. In the second chapter I have discussed the historical connect between Sanskrit and Manipuri. There are references in ancient Manipuri chronicles regarding several groups of immigrants who came from western part of India and other eastern countries. They took this route and settled here. The name Manipur was given to the state in the reign of king Garibnawaj (1708-48). Old historians and grammarians have a belief that present Manipur is the same Manipur which is discussed at several places in the Mahabharata.

In the third chapter I have taken up the phonology in both languages. Consonants b, d, g, j were not used in old Manipuri; p, t, k, c were used instead. Voiced aspirates bh, dh, gh, jh are the borrowed consonants from other languages like Sanskrit, Bengali, Hindi. As a result, many loan words from these languages, specially, Sanskrit have become the integral part of Manipuri. Intonation or accent is quite significant in Sanskrit. The position of the accent often decides the semantic value and grammatical function; we can see the difference from the words given below— 'gambhīranādaḥ (deep sound) is Karmadhāraya samāsa, where as gambhīranādaḥ (one having heavy voice) is considered as Bahuvrīhi.

The fourth chapter is about tense. The Benedictive Mood (āśīrliṅ) is a unique feature in Moods in Sanskrit. Tense is not very significant in Manipuri; in fact, modern scholars recognize Aspect in their grammatical system instead. Marker is added to the verb to tell different aspects.

The fifth chapter is regarding case. Manipuri language has one 'Associative Case'. Some grammarians do not include Dative in case category. To indicate the beneficiary, they apply 'da' marker which is also used in Locative Case. The provision of Double Case-Marker or Clitic shows the flexibility of Manipuri language.

In the sixth chapter I have discussed pronoun. In Manipuri there is no specific gender used for the third person pronoun; word 'mahāk' for singular and 'makhoy' for plural can depict all three genders. There are short forms for 'asmad' (first person) and 'yuṣmad' (second person) in some cases in Sanskrit, in Manipuri too'du' and 'si' are used as short forms in place of pronouns 'madu/adu' (that) and 'asi/masi' (this).

Compounds have been discussed in the seventh chapter. Compound is considered to be the most favourite ingredient of Sanskrit language, the speaker is at his/her liberty in compounding as many words as he/she desires. In Manipuri, compounds can be formed between nouns, noun and verb, verb and verb, noun and adjective. There are compounds consisting of three words also. In Sanskrit an indeclinable and a noun can be compounded, this compound is known as 'avyayībhāva samāsa'.

The eightth chapter is about Derivative Verbs. Derivatives are used in both languages, Causative and Desiderative verbs are found in both languages. In Manipuri, there are many suffixes which can be added to the verb to derive derivatives of different kinds; for example honorific suffixes, suffixes indicating superiority.

I believe that this work will enable students to explore the endless findings, yet to be further discovered and understood through the paths of Sanskrit and Manipuri languages.

4th February, 2014
Basant Panchami

Dr. A. Sudha Devi
Delhi

Acknowledgement

This book is a humble attempt in exploring the close connection between Sanskrit and Manipuri. As I began getting acquainted with Manipuri, my fascination for it grew more and more. The deep similarity in the systems of Sanskrit and Manipuri grammar further encouraged me towards a comparative study of both the languages.

The completion of this work would not have been so smooth without the voluntary help of Prof. Ch. Yashawanta Singh, Department of Linguistics, Manipur University. Being a close friend, he always made himself readily accessible in providing valuable suggestions and core material critical to my research. I shall always remain indebted to him. I thank the library staff of Manipur University, Imphal as well as the staff of Indira Gandhi Centre for Arts and Culture, Delhi for guiding me on the relevant resources comprising of books, journals on the subject matter. I am also thankful to the library staff, South Campus University of Delhi for making all the important material related to my work available to me while ignoring the overdue issuance of books. I am grateful to my husband's nephew, Mr. A.K. Ranjit Singh who never hesitated in sending across information, documents which were time and again needed by me from Manipur. I will always have fond affection for him. I am thankful to my husband Dr. A.K.Singh who introduced me to Manipuri and has been a constant motivating and driving force. His great support was indispensable towards the entire period of research and analysis.

My mother has been a great inspiration in my life, I am grateful to her for uncondional love towards me.

My family including my two daughters Mudita and Ruchira always boosted my morale and encouraged me in the long hours devoted towards the completion of this book.

Dr. A. Sudha Devi

Abbreviation

Abl.	Ablative
Act.	Active
Accom.	Accomplishment
Accus.	Accusative
Adj.	Adjective
Adv.	Adverb
Adv. Mark.	Adverbial marker
Ag.	Agent
Aor.	Aorist
Asp.	Aspect
Asso.	Associative
Bene.	Benedictive
Benef.	Benefactive
Catur.	Caturthī
Caus.	Causative
Ch.	Chapter
Comp.	Comparision
Con.	Connecting
Cond.	Condition
Conj.	Conjunction
Contr.	Contrast
Cop.	Copula
Corre. Pron.	Correlative pronoun
Dat.	Dative
Demons. Pron.	Demonstrative Pronoun
Deter.	Determiner
Dir.	Direct object
Distr. Pron.	Distributive Pronoun
Dvi.	Dvitīya

Emph.	Emphasis
Erg.	Ergative
Excl.	Exclusive
Expr.	Expression
Femi.	Feminine Gender
Fut.	Future
Genit.	Genitive Case
Imp.	Imperative
Imm.	Immediate
Incl.	Inclusive
Ind.	Indirect
Inde.	Indeclinable
Inde.Pron.	Indefinite Pronoun
Instr.	Instrumental
Int. Pron.	Interrogative Pronoun
Interj.	Interjection
Loc. Locat.	Locative
Mas. Gend.	Masculine Gender
MSS	Manuscript
Neg.	Negative
Neu. Gen.	Neuter Gender
Nom.	Nominative Case
NZR	Nominalizer
Obj.	Object
Pañca.	Pañcamī
Par.	Particle
Part.	Participle
Pas. Part.	Past Participle
Pass.	Passive
Perf.	Perfect
Peri.	Periphrastic Future
Pers.	Person
Pers. Pron.	Personal Pronoun
Pg.	Page

Plu. No.	Plural Number
Pot.	Potential
Poss. Pron.	Possessive Pronoun
Prath.	Prathamā
Pre.	Prefix
Prep.	Preposition
Pres.	Present Tense
Pro.	Progressive
Pron.	Pronoun
Pur.	Purpose
Ques.	Question
Reas.	Reason
Reci. Pron.	Reciprocal Pronoun
Ref. Pron.	Reflexive Pronoun
Rela. Pron.	Relative Pronoun
RV	Ṛgveda
Sapt.	Saptamī
Ṣaṣṭ.	Ṣaṣṭḥi
Sim.	Simple
Sing. no.	Singular Number
Soc.	Societive
Tr.	Transitive
Unr. Asp.	Unrealised Aspect
Unwan.	Unwanted
V. Tran.	Verb Trabsitive
Voc.	Vocative

Contents

I

Introduction

Sanskrit belongs to Indo-Aryan subgroup of Indo-European language group. In ancient time, Sanskrit was used in almost all over India, this has been established by many historical as well as archeological sources. Pāṇini refers to 'Prācām' (according to easterners) and 'Udīcām' (according to northerners). Here he is talking about different dialects of Sanskrit used in different parts of India. Kalidasa uses Sanskrit for educated and royal men and Prakrit (rustic Sanskrit) for women, illiterate and semi-literate men. The language used in two epics, the Ramayana and the Mahabharata is easy Spoken Sanskrit. The language of classical literature was grammatically rich and highly sanskritised but Buddha's teachings were in prakritised Sanskrit which became the lifeline of the masses, specially in northern India. Kushan kings used this prakritised Sanskrit as an official language for almost two centuries after Christian era.

Manipur is situated in the North-East of India, this place is known as one of the seven sisters of the North-East. It is a valley privileged with scenic beauty and surrounded by hills. In ancient times Manipur happened to be one of the routes for South Asia, South East Asia and Central Asia; as a result several ethnic groups which belonged to Southern Mongoloid, the Tibeto-Burman, the Indo-Aryan groups came to Manipur and made this land as their home. The people living in Manipur valley are known as the Meiteis and the people living in the surrounding hills are known as the Nagas and the Kuki-Chins; they are known as the main descendents of those groups.

Manipuri belongs to Tibeto-Burman group which is a subgroup of Sino-Tibetan language group. According to Grierson, it was a major literary language of the Kuki-Chin Naga group, but it did not have the characteristics of both the languages of the Kuki-Chin as well as the Naga group. Until before the advent of Hinduism in Manipur in the 18th century A.D., the Manipuri literature was written in Meitei Mayek or Old Manipuri script. Modern Manipuri or Bengali script came into existence only after the conversion of the religion of the Meitei or the Manipuri people. As a result, Bengali script became the main tool or medium of the official work of Manipuri establishment and literary work of the scholars. There is an opinion that even in 15th century A.D. under the rule of king Kiyamba, some Sanskrit scholars had come to Manipur and settled there. The linguistic, religious and cultural influence started showing its impact on Manipuri people since then. As a result, vocabularies and loan words not only from Sanskrit but also from Hindi, Bengali and Assamese started having place in Manipuri language and literature. As a next step, a lot of grammatical terms from Sanskrit and other languages were adopted in Manipuri. It is not surprising that many traditional grammarians have been great scholars of Sanskrit also. It is only in recent times that several modern grammarians and linguists have been engaged in propounding and establishing theories on various linguistic subjects like verb, tense, aspect, reduplication etc. of Manipuri language. Research scholars are constantly engaged in exploring various new dimensions in the linguistic areas of this language.

Manipuri is an agglutinating language, many suffixes can be added to the verbal root to depict different meanings. Root plays a significant role in Manipuri language. There are two types of roots— Free and Bound. Free roots are nominal roots. Bound roots are also two types— Nominal Bound root and Verbal Bound root.

1. Nominal Bound Roots—

Nominal Bound roots can not be used without personal pronominals, for example—

pā	i pā = ipā	ma pā = mapā
father	I father = my father	he/she father = father (his)

Nominal Bound Roots indicate complete meaning only when personal pronominal specially 3rd person pronominal is added to them. Mr. Grierson gives his observation about this arrangement— "There is a tendency to coin a separate word for every individual concrete conception.... For the word 'hand', 'foot' etc. they speak only of 'my hand, my foot."

2. Verbal roots are known as Dynamic and Stative Roots. Dynamic roots are action oriented, for example—

Cā = eat   pā = read

Roots like cāw = big, ṅaw = white are Stative Bound roots. Grammatical terms like nominal, adjective verb etc. can be derived by adding affixes to the Dynamic root.

In Sanskrit verb has two voices— active and passive. Active voice is denoted by 'parasmaipada' which indicates that the work is done for other person than the actor— pacati = cooks (for the other person). Active voice is also denoted by 'ātmanepada' that the doer is doing the action for himself or herself— pacate = cooks (for himself or herself), ātmanepada is also used in passive voice— pacyate = is being cooked. Some verbs are conjugated in parasmaipada, some in ātmanepada and there are some verbs which are derived in both.

In Manipuri there is no passive voice; as a result the roles of the verbs are fixed and cannot be manipulated syntactically. Traditional grammarians, though, have tried to establish that passive voice exists in Manipur, let us see the sentences below—

1. leirik   pūre.
   Book   bring/carry perf. asp.
   I   brought the book.

2. aṅgāṅ cayre.
Child scold perf. asp.

Mother or someone scolded the child.

They considered another type of syntax also as passive—

Bali ni	ram na	hātkhi	ba.
Bali (cop)	Ram erg.	kill perf.	nzr.

It is Bali that Ram killed.

Modern linguists do not recognize both types of sentences as passive.

In the first example the sentences are pro-drop type. The verbs retain their transitive form; the sentences are not able to denote the passive meaning. In the second example the sentences are complex, not passive. In passive the subject of active voice changes its position, but in this example the subject is still in the first position.

There are three persons, three genders and three numbers in Sanskrit. The genders of nouns do not have any specific rules which could be followed to differentiate from one to another. But the distinction becomes obvious by the natural difference in names of two male and female sexes— ajaḥ (male goat), ajā (female goat) or haṅsaḥ (male swan) and haṅsī (female swan). Sometimes three words in three genders can be seen for the same thing; dāraḥ (mas.), bhāryā (feminine), kalatram (neu.) depict the same meaning 'wife'. Similarly 'taṭaḥ, taṭī, taṭam tell the same word 'shore'. Word 'mitram' which means friend, is used in neuter gender and mitraḥ which means sun is used in masculine gender. There are three numbers in Sanskrit— singular, dual and plural. Besides indicating one person or thing, singular number also indicates the whole class— gauḥ (cow) or naraḥ (man) also indicates cow in general and man in general. The dual number indicates two as in 'tau' (two) or 'pitarau' (parents), but where pair or couple is indicated, the word takes singular— bāhudvayam (a pair of arms). The plural denotes more than two, but it may also indicate the whole class like singular— paśavaḥ (animals).

In Sanskrit there is a tradition to use plural for a person to show respect and reverence— ācāryāḥ (respected teacher) or bhavatyaḥ (you, madam). If a person belongs to a high position, then the first person singular is used in plural— vayamapi āgatāḥ (we/I have arrived).

When two or more nouns connected with **ca** (and) word are used as subject, the verb takes their combined number, for example—

rāmaḥ lakśmaṇaḥ sītā ca vanam jagmuḥ. (Ram Lakshmana and Sita went to forest.)

When nouns are taken separately in a sentence, the verb is used in a singular number— na mām trātum tātaḥ prabhavati na cāmbā na bhavatī. (Māl. 2.) (My father cannot save me, neither my mother nor you lady!)

Sometimes the verb is used according to the nearest subject, for example— ahaśca rātriśca ubhe ca sandhye dharmo'pi jānāti narasya vṛttam. (Day night, both twilights and Dharma also knows man's action.)

In Latin also thc samc arrangcmcnt is found— Filia ct unus a fitüs captus est. (A daughter and one of the sons was captured.)

When subjects are connected by **vā** (or) word, the verb takes singular number— nalinī śyāmā pavitrā vā idam pāṭham paṭhatu. (Let Nalini Shyama or Pavitra read this chapter.)

When subjects in different persons are used and the word **ca** (and) is connecting them, then the verb agrees with their combined number— tvam cāham vidyālayam gacchāvaḥ. (You and I are going to the school.)

In Manipuri, there are three persons, two genders— masculine and feminine. This differentiation is solely based on natural sexes, otherwise there are no grammatical genders. To differentiate between male and female among human beings, birds and animals, suffix pa/ba for male and pi/bi for female is added to the root— hurānba (thief) and hurānbi (thief female), yenba (cock) and yenbi (hen).

Manipuri has two numbers— singular and plural. No marker is used to indicate the singular number, for plural 'siṅ' or 'khoy' is added to the noun—

aṅgāṅ = child aṅgāṅ siṅ = children
Yāw = sheep yāw siṅ = sheep(s)

For animals, 'lāba' is used to indicate male and 'amom' is used to indicate female—

hui lāba = dog hui amom = bitch.

In Manipuri, 3rd person pronoun 'mahāk' indicates male and female both. For formal use in 2nd person, honorific pronouns like 'adom, asom or som' are used. In Sanskrit 'bhavān or bhavatī' words are used for male and female in formal address.

Manipuri Puyas which were written by Meiteis, became instrumental in highlighting the historical events and establishing the chronology of those events. These chronicles covered a period of almost 2000 years. Among many Puyas, Bamon Kunthok (The Immigration of Brahmins) is of great significance, this chronicle throws light on continuous inflow of Brahmin groups into Manipur and their conscious religious activities in ancient time.

In the later period the Gazetteers and Census became authentic source of information on history of Manipur, since they contained the reports of inquiries which were conducted in different fields in Manipur. Captain R.B. Pemberton in his Report on The Eastern Frontier of British India which was printed at Calcutta in 1835, gave elaborate and excellent description of the oppression by the Burmese and the condition of the inhabitants of the reconstituted State of Manipur. This report later helped in initiating operations to regain its independence. In 1840 Col. William Mc Culloch went to Manipur as Assistant Political Agent and was also Political Agent till 1867. He presented a very exhaustive information on Manipur and its people in his Account of the Valley of Munnipore, and of the Hill Tribes, with a comparative vocabulary of the Munnipore and other languages. This long period of twenty seven years gave him ample opportunity to understand Manipuri culture. Dr. D.R. Brown, also a Political Agent in Manipur wrote Statistical Account of Manipur which was printed by Government at Calcutta in 1874. This work is a confirmation of Mc Culloch's information. The Government distributed its copies largely. Mr. G.H. Damant was a Civil Servant, he wrote many papers on the history of Manipur, its archaic literature and the relation of various Indo-Chinese races with one another. His papers were published in Journals of the Asiatic Society of Bengal and The Royal Asiatic Society.

Dr. A. Sudha Devi

II

Historical connect between Sanskrit and Manipuri

Language is the medium of communication. Languages evolve and diversify over a period of time. Human language can be productive and diminutive because of its involvement with social convention and learning.

Manipuri is the language/Lingua Franca of the people of Manipur in the north-east of India; there are 33 dialects spoken in this land. Manipur lies between Latitude 23.80° to 25.68° North and Longitude 93.03° to 94.78° East. Its total area is 22,327 sq. Km. It is surrounded by Nagaland on the north, Assam on the west and Mizoram on the south, it shares a 398 Km. long international boundary with Myanmar. The three major groups of people inhabited in Manipur are the Meities of the valley, the Nagas and the Kuki Chins of the hilly area. The languages spoken by these people come in the category of Tibeto-Burman Languages. The Tibeto-Burman language family comprises of most widely spoken Burmese and the Tibetic languages. People of Manipur valley speak Manipuri which falls in TB language group. After much deliberation and debate, it was included in schedule viii languages of India in the year 1992. According to S. K. Chatterjee, "Among the Tibeto-Burman languages, the most and in literature certainly of much greater importance than the others is the Meitei or Manipuri language."[1]

The name Manipur which means 'land of gems' was officially given to this land in the period 1709-1748 A.D. during the reign of the ruler Pamheiba, a Naga chief, who was known as king Garibnawaz (patron of the poor), after he got converted to Hinduism. Before this, Manipur was known by different names by people of different places; Meklee by Assamees, Moglie by Cacharis, Kathe by Burmese etc. It is evident from the ancient coins that king Garibnawaz was known as 'Mekhleshwar' and the kingdom as 'Mekhla'. During his rule, a priest named Santadas Adhikari (Gošai) from Narasingh Tilla of Sylhet persuaded Garibnawaz to convert to Vaishnavism of Ramananda Sect. The king was so much impressed by his preaching about Hinduism that he took up a mission of converting the whole state into a Hindu place. He ruthlessly curbed the protests of the priests and people who insisted on following their own religion. He got so much influenced by this Santadas that he got a large number of scriptures and valuable books burnt in public. This way valuable literature and historical evidences were lost for ever. After this, Hinduism spread in two folds— temples were constructed with idols of Rama-Sita, Radha-Krishna and other gods; at the same time Sanskrit literature like the Ramayana, the Mahabharata, the Bhagvdgita and various Puranas was translated into Manipuri language. After some protest, people started practising Vaishnavism but they practiced their own religion also.

Vaishnavism reached its glory in the period of king Bhagyachandra who had succeeded Garibnawaz. In 1780 A.D. he constructed an image of Gobindjee out of a tree from Kaina hill. It is said that he had a vision and that he was inspired to compose Ras Leela which was considered to be the greatest devotional expression to lord Krishna in Manipur. Later in the nineteenth century, king Gambhira Singh and his son contributed to the spread of Vaishnavism in Manipur. Hinduism in the form of Vishnuswami sect, Madhva sect, Nimbarka sect etc. flourished side by side in Manipur. But the Manipuris embraced Chaitanya sect more happily because in the worship of Radha-Krishna, Sankirtana was the main part of devotion in this cult. They imbibed it into their culture very deeply. During Sankirtanas, they would get so much involved in the devotion that they would cry and shed tears. King

Artists performing Manipuri Sankirtana

Charairongba, father of king Garibnawaz followed Gaudiya Vaishnavism. In Sh. Jhalajit Singh's words, "Sri Krishna is the principal God from whom other incarnations emanate. He is the supreme reality in the system of Charairongba time."[2] The impact of Hinduism in Manipur started reflecting in socio-political system, rituals, religious practices and literary works also. Caste system started settling in, which did not exist before. The Meiteis were classed as Kshatriyas and people who migrated from western India, were known as Brahmans or Bamons. The gotra system followed soon. A line of royal descendence known as Vanshavali was prepared on the basis of mythical connection with Sages. The seven Salais of the Meitei clans were identified with Hindu gotras.

This conversion of religion became a big reason for the import of Sanskrit, Bengali and Hindi words into Manipuri language. The linguistic similarity could not be a mere co-incidence. Loan words from other languages come in a language after a long contact with the people, speaking those languages. Structural similarity between two languages occurs when one language has influenced another language for quite a long period.

Scholars like Sanajaoba establish the traces of Hinduism in the Manipuri society even before 18th century. An ancient Vishnu temple which is situated in Bishnupur, was erected during the rule of king Kyamba (1467-1508). The Vishnu idol seated on Garuda, was presented to the king by Tswaba Khekhomba, the Shan king of Pong. In 1697 A.D.king Charairongba, known as Gopal Singh who was the father of Garibnawaz, started worshipping the idols of Radha-Krishna. He had in fact, installed these idols which can be seen even today.[3]

Manipuri Puyas are the historical chronicles. Many important Puyas were destroyed by king Garibnawaz in the wake of Hinduisation in Manipur. But local people managed to preserve some of them secretly; hence they are available today to throw light on the historical events of old

18th Century coins written in Sanskrit

times. These Puyas contain systematic historical events. Cheitharol Kumbaba, one of the Puyas, is known to be the most authentic and accurate chronicle. It throws light on royal lineage, socio-political and cultural development of Manipur. This state chronicle was recorded by learned Maichus (Pundits) in the original Manipuri script. It covers the historical events of about 2000 years, starting from king Lairen Pakhangba (A.D.33-154) to Bodh Chandra Singh (A.D.1941-1955), hence covering the rule of about 78 kings. According to this chronicle, Vaishnavism started cementing its base mainly in the 18th century. The chronicle states, "There was a great movement of Nitainand Dharma (Chaitanya Nityananda Dharma or Gauda Dharma) in 1737-38 in Manipur. Three thousand people were initiated into the new faith everyday."[4]

Among other puyas, there is one Bamon Kunthok (the immigration of Brahmins), which provides details of socio -cultural transformation of the people of Manipur in the 17th century. This chronicle provides vast information about the immigration of Brahmin groups to Manipur and their religious activities. In this context it will only be relevant to quote Mr. T.C. Hodson, "— the records of the Brahmin families in Manipur claim in some cases that the founder of the family settled in the valley at so remote a date as the middle of the fifteenth century".[5]

There is another Puya named Nongchup Haram which also provides information about the immigration from the west to Manipur.

Aryan Traces—

The archeological study done by some historians establishes the impact of Hinduism on Manipuri society even before 14th or 15th century A.D. Some western scholars like Captain Dun , Dr. D.R.Brown have tried to establish the theory of Aryan inflow in Manipur before 14th or 15th century. Dun observes , "There can be no reasonable doubt that a great Aryan wave of very pure blood passed through Manipur into Burma in pre-historic times. I see traces of this in the finely cut features seen now and then among the Manipuris."[6] It may be noted that general facial features of the Manipuris are Mongoloid types. Dr. D. R. Brown in his Statistical Account of Munnipore also expresses the same views. The features of some of the Manipuris show the Aryan resemblance. Their features are not as sharp as those of pure Aryan race but certainly different from the original Mongoloid type.

There are several Indian scholars like W. Yumjao Singh, R.K. Jhalajit, Sanajaoba who also propound the theory of Aryan origin of the Manipuri. W. Yumjao Singh has talked about a copper plate, named 'Phayeng Copper Plate'. It is written in Meitei Mayek (the original Manipuri script) and he claims its period to be around 799 A.D. This plate was inscribed under the rule of king Khongtekcha. The inscription begins with Shri Hari and refers to Shiva, Durga, Ganesha and other gods. This indicates that the king regarded Hari as the Supreme Being.[7] He also talks about another plate of the same period which suggests the possibility of practice of Shaivism at that time. S.N. Parrat is of completely different view, he believes that this plate could be of not earlier period than the 19th century.[8] Few rectangular coins, which were issued by different rulers, have been found written in Devanagari script. Some scholars have tried to establish the period of these coins as early as 33—154 A.D. during the reign of Pakhangba but it is still a subject of debate.

A large number of historians like S.N. Parrat, Gangmumei Kabui, R.B. Pemberton and many modern linguists like Ch. Yashwanta Singh do believe that Meiteis (Manipuris) do not have Aryan origin and that they are purely of Mongoloid descent. According to them, it was the handiwork of Brahmanic missionaries to establish the Aryan origin of Manipuris which was supported by royal patronage and a certain class of people. Gangmumei Kabui gives his observation, "The origin of the Meiteis is not of Aryan, there is an Aryan element in the Meitei society." Further he says, "—many Aryan colonizers, adventurers, immigrants came to Manipur or passed through this land...... in course of their colonization or trade with west China and south east Asia as Manipur was on the route of trades and immigration..."[9]

The enforcement of Hinduism had a great impact on Manipuri life but the people retained their original religion also. Some western scholars find the Meiteis as the descendents of the hill tribes, because of the cultural and linguistic affinity between them and the Meiteis. R.B. Pemberton, who is regarded as the pioneer of modern historical researches in Manipur, observes that Manipuris are of the Tartar origin of China,[10] though this observation of Pemberton is not acknowledged by other scholars.

After studying the observations of different scholars, establishing the Aryan origin of Manipuris will be just hypothetical. It is justified to reach the conclusion that Manipur was on the way of traders from east as well as west, so these traders halted there, stayed for as long as it suited to them and even settled there for life. With the result, Manipuris absorbed elements of foreign culture and language which came in their contact with time. The two

Puyas namely, Nongpok Haram and Nongchup Haram are indeed the great documentary evidences in this context. Nongpok Haram throws light on the eastern immigrants, similarly Nongchup Haram discusses about the western immigrants into Manipur. People coming from the east were Tibeto-Burmans, Tai (Shans), Chinese etc. The people, who came from the west, were Bamons or Brahmins, Bengalis, Muslims, Kacharis, Bishnupuriyas etc. The history of Manipur indicates that people from the west, having Indo-Aryan blood, came to Manipur much later than the people from the eastern side. The dating system in Manipur by Shakabda era was introduced quite late, possibly in reign of Garibnawaz. Before that, the dating method was through 'Cheithaba' (counting of sticks). One may be surprised by the accuracy of this system. In Saroj Parrat's words,"Kyamba's (Sak1389-1430) 'Cheithapa' dating system is so meticulous that it would have been quite superfluous to have introduced a second system of dating (Sakabda) alongside it".[11] There is a Ningel inscription of king Garibnawaz which was recorded in Cheithaba year (Saka 1658) in the reign of Garibnawaz. Ningel was a small town in Thoubal district in Manipur. It has thirteen lines and it starts with 'jaya sri garibanawaz,' even though it was written in archaic Manipuri. The time of the historical evidences like coins or excavated idols of different Hindu deities or inscriptions may be a subject of debate but this also indicates the inflow of western traders and immigrants in Manipur from an early period .

Since early times, Manipur has been an enterprising route for people of other parts of India. There were hill routes which connected Manipur with the Surma valley, the Brahmaputra valley and the Kabaw valley. The Kabaw valley lies on the Indo-Burma border on one side and the Ningthee river (Chindvin river) on the other side. Many Aryan colonizers, settlers passed through these routes, stayed there as long as they wanted and moved to Burma. Some of them settled there for ever. Mr. D.G.E. Hall mentions about a road connecting Lower Burma with India via the bank of the Irawadi, the bank of Chindwin and Manipur.[12] The Buddhist Missionaries also took these hill routes to reach China for propagating Buddhism.

Manipur of the Mahabharata—

In the Mahabharata there are references that Arjuna visited Manipur, married Chitrangada, the daughter of Chitravahana who was the king of Manipur. He had a son from Chitrangada named Babhruvahana. Arjuna stayed there for three years and after that he left for the south. Babhruvahana became the king after his grandfather's death. During Aśvamedha campaign, Arjuna again visited Manipur. There was a fierce battle between father and son, the father was killed but later he was revived by the son. Then Chitrangada went to Hastinapur along with the son to attend the Aśvamedha Yajña.

In the Ādi Parva there is a reference that after having violated the rule with his elder brother, Arjuna went in self-exile for twelve years. During this period he wandered extensively and saw the whole of India, he went to Manipur also; the śloka says—

'Mahendraparvatān dṛṣṭvā tapasairupaśobhitam
samudratīreṇa śanairmaṇipuram jagāma ha.
(ādi parva, ch. 215, śloka 13)

After seeing Mahendraparvat, Arjuna went to Manipur by the sea side. Before going to Manipur he had seen Kalinga which is in Orissa, this is evident from the following śloka—

'sa kaliṅgānatikramya deśānāyatanāni ca
vanāni ramaṇīyāni prekśamāṇo yayau prabhuḥ.
(ādi parva ch.215, śloka 12)

Some scholars like L. Iboongohal Singh, R.K.Jhalajit, W.Yumjao Singh are strong believers of the view that this Manipur is the same Manipur which is referred in the Mahabharata at several places. To support this view, they put forth the arguement that Arjuna desired to see the east—

'prācīnadiśābhiprepsur jagāma'——.

Arjuna passed through Kalinga after seeing Mahendra parvat. According to them, he could not possibly go to Ganjam which lies in the Deccan. Since Arjuna wanted to see the east first, so he went to Manipur. East lies on the latitude of 24° North and longitude of 94.47° east. This indicates the location of Manipur.

During Aśvamedha campaign, Arjuna went to Manipur after defeating the king of Trigarte (modern Jullundhar), he also fought with the ruler of Pragjyotisha (Kamarupa in Assam). The reference is—

Krameṇa sa hayastvevam vicaran bharatarṣabha
Maṇipūrapaterdeśamupāyāt saḥ pāṇḍavaḥ.
(Aśvamedha parva, ch. 77, śloka 46).

After having reconciled with his son, Babhruvahana in Manipur, Arjuna went to Magadha (Bihar), had a battle with the ruler of Rajagriha (the capital). The śloka says—

Anugacchañśca tejasvī nivṛtto 'tha kirīṭabhṛt
Yadṛcchayā samāpede puram Rajagṛham tadā.
(aśvamedha parva, ch.83, śloka 2)

After this, he went to Vanga, Punḍra and Kerala—

'tato yatheṣṭamagamat punareva sa kesarī
tataḥ samudratīreṇa vaṅgānpuṇḍrān sa keralān.'
(aśvamedha parva, ch.84, śloka 29)

After carefully studying the route shown in the above ślokas regarding the invasion of Arjuna— Jullundhar, Assam and Manipur and way back to the south via Magadha, the view for present Manipur being the same Manipur as referred in the Mahabharata gets stronger. In support of this view, the argument is that if the Mahabharata Manipur is located on the seaside near Kalinga, then on the route from there to either south or Hastinapur, Magadha which is referred in the epic could not be touched.

Lastly in the Mahaprasthanika Parva there is a reference that Chitrangada returned to Manipur with her son and the Pandavas and Draupadi left Hastinapur for heaven—

Chitrāṅgadā yayau cāpi maṇipūrapuram prati
Śiṣṭāḥ parīkśitam tvanyā mātaraḥ paryavārayaṇ.
Pāṇḍavāśca mahātmāno draupadi ca yaśasvinī
Kṛtopavāsāḥ kauravya prayayuḥ prāṅmukhāstataḥ.
(mahāprasthānika parva, ch. 1 śloka 26, 27)

Regarding the location of the Mahabharata Manipur near seashore, the scholars, in support of the Mahabharata connect present the logic that the Mahabharata was written about 2000 years b. c .It is possible that the present Manipur was near seashore at that time and during the upheaval this mountainous change occurred. [13]

A large number of scholars do not agree with this view, their argument is that since Manipur of the Mahabharata was situated by the side of the sea, somewhere near Kalinga (Orissa), hence that cannot be identified with the modern Manipur which is far away from the sea-coast. Although R.C. Majumdar is a great exponent of the Aryan theory, but he also does not relate the Mahabharata Manipur to the present Manipur.[14] The legend of Arjuna and Chitrangada is known all over India, so it was a natural effort of linking present Manipur with the Mahabharata Manipur.

It is believed that it was Shanti Das Goswami from Bengal who had attempted to establish the present Manipur to be the Manipur of the Mahabharata. Therefore, this Sanskrit name Manipur was given recognition in the eighteenth century, during the rule of Garib Nawaz. This was the time of the spread of Hinduism and the pivotal role in this regard was played by the Goswami. In the views of Naorem Sanajaoba , "In the pre-Garib Nawaz inscriptions of Kanthonjam Lairemma not a single Sanskritised word occurred. Even the inscription of Charairengba, the father of Garib Nawaz was not occurred by Sanskritised word."[15] Historically, nowhere in Manipuri Chronicles, MSS and other literary works, this land is found to be referred as Manipur. In no Manipuri folklores and fables has this Manipur name occurred for once. This land was known in different periods by different names. The people of Manipur divided the millennium in Chaks. In Hayi Chak; the first millennium, the land was called 'Tillikoktong Ahanba'. In Haya Chak; second millennium, she was known as 'Mira Pongthoklam. In Khunnung Chak; third millennium as Hanna Samba Konna Loiba, in early Konna Chak; early fourth millennium she was known as Muwapali Mayai Sumtongpam and in later Konna Chak this land was popularly known as 'Kanglei Pungmayol, Kangleipak and Meitrapak. Manipur was known by other names also, such as; Chakpa Langba, Muwapali,Wangam Tengthong, Mayung Kuiba Lengthong, Maphei Pakpa and later on as Poirei Meitei after the arrival of Poireiton.

The Connection between Sanskrit and Manipuri Words—

Apart from the possible closeness among Aryans from the western India and the tribes of Manipur from the pre-historic times, there is found to be a very very close connection between Sanskrit and Manipuri words. Many scholars, who have been working tirelessly on history of Manipur, have come across a great number of words which have so much similarity with Sanskrit words that one may be bound to draw a conclusion that these words were borrowed from Sanskrit quite long ago; much before 17th century.

From the list mentioned below, one can notice that some of the Sanskrit words used in Manipuri language, are still in their original form, whereas some words have gone through a phonetic change with time.

Sanskrit	Manipuri	English
golokaḥ	korau	Heaven
śyālakaḥ	selau	Brother-in-law
pālakaḥ	phalau	Protector

śṛṅgam	ciṅ	Mountain
śṛṅgaveram	siṅ	Ginger
mastakam	makok or matok	Head or Forehead
swarṇa	sanā	Gold (volgarian—sureń /sareń)
premā	pemā	an affectionate girl
nāman	namiṅ	name (your name)
nitya	nuti	Everyday
ayaḥ	yot	Iron
arkaḥ	aṅkot	a plant
prāṇaḥ	pān	breathing, living
taraṅgaḥ	taraṅg	Wave
kśayaḥ	kham	to end
ched	chet	to tear
puya	pum	to rot, in Sanskrit it means Pus from a wound
surendraḥ	sorāren	Indra/sky-god
ravaḥ	yava	Sound-voice
buddhi	pothi	Intelligence
bukkaḥ	puk/buk	Stomach
ādityaḥ	atiya	Sun (in Manipuri it means sky, may be because the sun is in the sky)
koṇaḥ	kona	Angle
sthā	thāba	to plant
nyāyaḥ	ningei	justice/argument
swakīyaḥ	sagei	Relative
jahaḥ	Cā	Son or daughter, Nighaṇṭu–Jahaḥ apatyanāmāni

In the above list of words we find a pattern in change of voiced to voiceless consonants. Manipuri words 'asi' and 'adu' have great similarity to Sanskrit pronouns; 'asmin' and 'adas' but in different meaning. Word 'asi' means 'this' and Sanskrit word 'asmin' means 'in this' which is the viith case (locative). It is assumed that with time, this phonetic change occurred having some different analogy which is visible between words 'asi' and 'asmin'. One may come across a great number of such Manipuri words which might have originated from Sanskrit, but with due course of time, mixing with a different society speaking different language; words with some phonetic change, started giving completely different meaning.

Some examples of false analogy are being discussed here. Sanskrit word 'ghuṭ' means 'knee', there is a similar Manipuri word 'khud' which means 'hand'. Another Sanskrit word 'ahan' means 'day', but the Manipuri word 'ahing' gives absolutely different meaning 'night.' Both these examples are indicative that the original Sanskrit word started corresponding a completely different meaning in a period of time. Change of meaning does occur over a long period.

Next, we will examine the phonetic development of some words which have great identity with Sanskrit words. The word 'āha' in Sanskrit means 'to say', in Manipuri it is 'hāi̯'. Generally ending phoneme 'i' in a verb indicates present tense. With time this 'i' might have become an integral part of the word 'hāi'. Manipuri word 'tau' which means 'do', might have originated from Sanskrit verb 'stu' which means 'worship'. Incidentally, according to Max Muller English verb 'do' originated from Sanskrit root 'dhā'— to hold. One may assume that the Manipuris chose Sanskrit verb 'stu'— worship for the verb 'tau'—'do', because in every action they did, they thought it as a worship to God , be it regarding eating, bathing, sleeping etc.

Another great Sanskrit connection with Manipuri language is reflected, while dealing with compound words.

The name for the sun in old Manipuri language is 'tāodanba' or 'tāotanba'— the thing which moves in the sky. This word is constructed of two words— tāo + tamba; 'tāo' means sky in Manipuri. In Sanskrit 'dyu' word means 'sky' and 'tamba' root means 'to go' or 'to move'. In Manipuri 'cakmom' word is used for 'fire', we can trace its roots in Sanskrit word 'yajñamayaḥ'. In fact the literal meaning of 'yajñamayaḥ' is a fire to which some offering is done. It is significant to learn that despite Sanskrit language having so many words meaning 'fire', people from Manipur chose 'yajñamayaḥ' and used it as 'cakmom'. It indicates that they treated 'fire' as sacred and always to be worshipped. The Avestan word for fire is 'yasna'. The word 'thambāl' in Manipuri means 'lotus'. It is a compound word having two words; 'tham' and 'bāl'/'pān'. 'Pān' means flower and 'tham' word is related to lotus; any part of lotus. 'Thamna' is used for lotus leaf, 'thamjet' means lotus fruit and 'thambau' means lotus root. Lotus in Sanskrit is meant by 'padma'. In many parts of India, this 'padma' word is pronounced as 'padam'. In Manipur too, this 'padma' word, having been contracted to 'padam', then possibly to 'dam' (pa no more in use) took the form of ' tham'. Hence, the word 'thambāl' came in practice.

A house is called 'yum' in Manipuri, whereas 'gṛham' is the word in Sanskrit. In Pali 'giyom' means a house. It may be noted that Buddhist temples in Manipur are known as 'kiyong'. This 'kiyong' word changed from 'giyom'. 'Giyom' might have originated from 'gṛham'. In old Manipuri, 'yom' word was used for 'house'. It is evident that 'o' in 'yom' converted to 'u' in 'yum' which is in use in present day. In Latin 'domus' means house. Sanskrit word for ear is 'karṇa' and for nose is 'nāsā' or 'nāsikā'. In Manipuri, words 'nākoṅg' and 'nā' mean ear, similarly word 'nāton' means nose. The interesting thing is that both 'nākoṅg' and 'nāton' words have 'nā' in common. If we follow the linguistic formula then the word 'karṇa' would change to 'koṅgna', but we see that it changed to 'nākoṅg', by further contraction it remained as 'nā'. In Vedic literature, 'rayim' word has been used for 'wealth'. The same word with the same meaning has been in use in old Manipuri language. In Latin 'res' word means wealth/property. Sanskrit word 'rājendra' has same denotation in Manipuri word 'lāyren'. 'Rajendra' has two words; rājā + indra which means king of kings or lord of kings. In 'lāyren' word also 'lāy' means king or God and 'ren' means chief or king; hence king of kings. In Iranian word 'ri' means king. 'Sthaga' word in Sanskrit means a cheat or a rogue. The Prakrit word for it is 'thaga'. The Manipuri word corresponding the same meaning is 'thok'; thok touba means 'to cheat'. 'Tubi' word in Manipuri means lord or protector of the masses, this word is synonymous to 'lāyren'. This 'tubi' word can be traced even in Vedas—

"kavino mitrāvaruṇā tubi jāta urukśhya

das'āng dadhāpo apasam. (RV.I.II.IX).

May Mitrāvaruṇa who is born in tubi jāta (as the protector of the masses), who has many abodes, who has intellect; enrich our energy and strength.

Manipuri word 'thu' or 'thou/thuba' means to hasten; to rush. In Sanskrit 'dru' root gives the same meaning; hence it can be assumed that this 'thu' word originated from Sanskrit root 'dru'.

Such close affinity in Sanskrit and Manipuri leads us to conclude that there has been a long connection between these two languages and that it is not merely a chance or a coincidence. Aryan traders and settlers passed through Manipur for going to China, Burma or south-east Asia since ancient time and in the process they settled here. With the result, Manipuri culture absorbed Aryan culture and the linguistic similarity between Sanskrit and Manipuri language occured subsequently.

Footnotes—

1. The Mongoloids and Their Contribution to the History and Culture of India pg. 157

2. History of Manipur pg. 116
3. Manipur: Past and Present pp. 163, 164
4. The Lost Kingdom; Royal Chronicle of Manipur— L. Joychandra Singh pg. v.
5. The Meiteis pg. 95
6. Gazetter of Manipur
7. Report on the Archeological Studies of Manipur, Bulletin no.1
8. The Religion of Manipur pp. 107-109
9. History of Manipur pg. 13, 15 and 16.
10. Eastern Frontier of India pg. 36
11. The Court Chronicle of the King of Manipur, Cheitharol Kumbaba pg. 5
12. History of South East Asia pg. 121
13. L. Iboongohal Singh— History of Manipur pg. 57
14. Refer Gangmumei Kabui— Land and People pg. 5
15. Manipur: Past and Present pg.158

III. 1

Phonology in Sanskrit

Phonology is a linguistic aspect which deals with the study of speech sound in a given language or across languages. According to Wikipedia, "Phonology is the systemic use of sound to encode meaning in any spoken language or the field of linguistics studying this use."

Sanskrit is written in Devnāgari script in most parts of India but in states like Bengal, Chennai, Kerala, Manipur etc. it is also written in the native script. Word **deva** means god in Sanskrit, this word originated from **div** root in the meaning of 'shine'— indicating Aryans who had fairer complexion as compared to the aborigines of India. Word **nāgari** means settlement, hence Devnāgari hints at the language of Aryans who had come to India from the northern side and settled there. Devnāgari script has been used in India since the rule of As'oka around 3rd century B.C. Inscriptions containing his edicts are written in Nāgari script only. There are 46 letters in this alphabet, consisting of 13 vowels and 33 consonants.

Vowels—	a	अ	ā	आ	i	इ	ī	ई		
	u	उ	ū	ऊ	ṛ	ऋ	ṛṛ	ॠ		
	lṛ	लृ	e	ए	ai	ऐ	o	ओ		
	au	औ								
Consonants—	k	क	kh	ख	g	ग	gh	घ	ṅ	ङ
	c	च	ch	छ	j	ज	jh	झ	ñ	ञ
	ṭ	ट	ṭh	ठ	ḍ	ड	ḍh	ढ	ṇ	ण
	t	त	th	थ	d	द	dh	ध	n	न
	p	प	ph	फ	b	ब	bh	भ	m	म
	y	य	r	र	l	ल	v	व	ś	श
	ṣ	ष	s	स	h	ह				

1. (a) There are two nasal sounds— anusvāra and anunāsika, which may be used with vowels. The **anusvāra** is indicated by a dot above the letter— कंस: (Kaṅsaḥ). Anunāsika is indicated by a dot within a semi circle (ardhacandra) above the letter— कस्मिँश्चित् (kasmiṅścit).

   (b) Two vertical dots known as visarga are also used with vowels; this sign indicates the strong spirant sound. This visarga is placed after the letter and generally in the end of the word— रवि: (Raviḥ).

   (c) In Sanskrit the **avagraha** is the form of ऽ, which is used in a word following **e** or **o**, this indicates the omission of **a**— रामोऽस्ति (Rāmo'sti).

   (d) In Sanskrit there are three types of tones or accent pitches— udātta (higher or acute), anudātta (grave) and svarita or circumflex. This tone pattern has been observed in Vedic literature mainly, it is not seen in practice in classical or modern literature. The **udātta** has no mark, the **anudātta** is indicated by a horizontal line under the syllable and the **svarita** is indicated by a vertical line on the syllable. The **svarita** is used as a combination of an acute vowel followed by a grave vowel into a syllable. The vowel can be used as it is, in the beginning of a word or a sentence, but not when preceded by a consonant, e.g. apratykśam, aśvaḥ. Short **a** does not have a separate sign, when it follows a consonant in a word—रथ: (Rathaḥ).

2. (a) A consonant when used without any vowel, is indicated by a nether stroke underneath; पुस्तकम् (pustakam).

   (b) When two or more consonants are used in a word jointly, the last consonant takes the vowel and the preceding consonant is used without a nether and the vertical line; **pta** (प्त) in **sapta** (सप्त) or **ñcu** (ञ्चु)

in **cañcuḥ** (चञ्चुः).

(c) The consonant **r** if followed by a nether consonant or vowel **ṛ**, changes to sign ॅ which is placed above the following consonant— अर्कः (arkaḥ), प्रार्णम् (prārṇam).

Vowels—

1. Vowels are divided into two types—

(i) Short vowels—	a	अ	i	इ	u	उ
	ṛ	ऋ	lṛ	लृ		
(ii) Long vowels—	ā	आ	ī	ई	ū	ऊ
	ṝ	ॠ	e	ए	ai	ऐ
	o	ओ	au	औ		

There is one more type— protracted which is known as **pluta**, generally this type of vowel is not used in modern Sanskrit.

2. There is another classification of these vowels—

(i) Simple—	a	अ	ā	आ	i	इ
	ī	ई	u	उ	ū	ऊ
	ṛ	ऋ	ṝ	ॠ	lṛ	लृ
(ii) Diphthongs—	e	ए	ai	ऐ	o	ओ
	au	औ				

These diphthongs are known as sandhyakśaras in Prātiśākhyas which are formed by joining vowels—

e — a + i

o — a + u

ai — ā + i

au — ā + u

3. Short vowels when preceding a conjunct consonant, are treated as prosodially long vowels.

4. Among the diphthong vowels **e**, **o** are known as Guṇa

and **ai** , **au** as Vṛddhi.

5. Vowels **e**, **o** can be independently long, they can also be developed out of the combination of short vowels— a + i, a + u; Similarly vowels ai, au can be taken independently and they can be developed from vowels— a/ā + e, a/ā + o. Vowel **a** is also termed as Guṇa when it is produced from the combination of a+ṛ and it becomes **ar**, similarly, vowel **ā** is termed as Vṛddhi when it is produced from ā + ṛ and it becomes ār.

Articulatory System of Vowels and Consonant

	Unas-pirate	*asp-irate*	*unas-pirate*	*aspi-rate*	*na-sal*	*Semi vowel*	*sibil-ants*	*Simple vowel*	*Diph-thong*
gutturals	k	kh	g	gh	ṅ		Jiv. :	a, ā	e
palatal	c	ch	j	jh	ñ	y	ś	i, ī	ai
lingual	ṭ	ṭh	ḍ	ḍh	ṇ	r	ṣ	ṛ, ṛṛ	o
dental	t	th	d	dh	n	l	s	lṛ	au
labial	p	ph	b	bh	m	v/w	Up. :	u,ū	

6. In the sibilant division two dots are shown at two places. The first dots are known as jihvāmūlīya, they are used as half visarga before the pronunciation of k and kh. The second dots are termed as upadhmānīya, they are used as half visarga before the pronunciation of p and ph.

7. All the consonants are pronounced with a vowel when used independently, but while writing, a nether stroke is used with each.

8. The four semi-vowels y,r,l,v originate from i, u, ṛ, ḷ respectively.

9. In Sanskrit a simple **a varṇa** represents both a and ā.

10. First two consonants of all 5 groups and sibilants ś, ṣ, s and : are termed as Hard or Surd and the rest of the consonants, vowels, semi-vowels and h are termed as

Soft or Sonant.

11. The letters, which are pronounced from same places in the throat and take same effort are known as **'savarṇa'** or homogenous and those letters which are pronounced from different parts in the throat and take different efforts are known as **'asavarṇa'** or heterogeneous.

12. The letters kś and jñ are conjoined letters of k + ś and j + ñ respectively and they are always used in this way only.

13. A pause or **virāma** comes at the completion of the sentence or at the end of half śloka in the form of a vertical line (।), two vertical lines are used at the completion of a śloka. Euphony or sandhi is an important aspect of Sanskrit language.

Rules of Beginning and Ending of Words—

1. A word other than a verbal root or a nominal base may end at any vowel except **ṛ** and **ḷṛ** when used independently or in the end of a sentence. It may also take any of the consonants mentioned ahead; k ṭ t p ṅ ṇ n m l and even visarga at the end.

2. A word if used alone or at the beginning of a sentence, may start with any vowel or consonant but not the last letter of 5 groups of consonants and not even anunāsika or visarga.

3. Words can not take more than one consonant at the end except in the case of words with conjunct consonants like arkaḥ, sarpaḥ etc.

4. Visarga can occur only after a vowel in the end of a word and also medially before an unvoiced non-dental and non-retroflex.

5. New words can be derived by adding affixes to the root or word.

Common Consonant Clusters—

There is a great number of conjunct consonants which are used frequently in Sanskrit; kka, kta, khya, pta, ptra, gdha, gya, gna, ghra, gdha, chha, sva and many more. Sometimes four or five consonants are also used in conjunction— dbhya, rtsnya etc.

Euphony or Sandhi—

Sandhi or Samhitā occurs between the final and initial letters of two words, it also happens between a preposition and a root.

Svara Sandhi or Coalescence in Final and Initial Vowels—

In svara sandhi, the vowels—the final of the previous word and the initial of the succeeding word are joined together. The combined vowel may take the form of a similar long or a diphthong or a semi-vowel.

(a) When a simple short or long vowel is succeeded by a similar short or long vowel, they both become a long vowel, for example—

(i)	daitya	+	ariḥ	=	daityāriḥ
	Demon	+	enemy	=	Vishnu
(ii)	rājā	+	ājñā	=	rājājñā
	King	+	order	=	king's order
(iii)	kapi	+	īśaḥ	=	kapīśaḥ
	Monkey	+	lord	=	monkey god
(iv)	bhānu	+	udayaḥ	=	bhānūdayaḥ
	Sun	+	rise	=	sunrise
(v)	hotṛ	+	ṛkāraḥ	=	hotṛṛkāraḥ
	Priest	+	ṛkāra	=	priest's pronunciation of ṛ

This Sandhi is known as **dīrgha** sandhi.

(b) When final **a** or **ā** is followed by an initial **i, ī** or **u, ū,** they both become **e** and **o** respectively—

(i)	sura	+	indraḥ	=	surendraḥ
	god	+	lord	=	lord of gods
(ii)	nara	+	īśaḥ	=	nareśaḥ
	Man	+	lord	=	king
(iii)	hita	+	upadeśaḥ	=	hitopadeśaḥ
	Friendly	+	advice	=	friendly advice

If **a** or **ā** is followed by **ṛ**, **ṛṛ** or **lṛ**, then both letters change to **ar** and **al** respectively—

(i)	sapta	+	ṛṣiḥ	=	saptarṣiḥ
	Seven	+	sage	=	celestial or seven sages
(ii)	mahā	+	ṛṣiḥ	=	maharṣiḥ
	Great	+	sage	=	the great sage
(iii)	tava	+	lṛkāraḥ	=	tavalkāraḥ
	Your	+	lṛkāra	=	your pronunciation of lṛ

This is known as **guṇa** sandhi.

(c) When **a**, **ā** precedes **e**, **ai** or **o**, **au**, they both become **ai** and **au** respectively, for example—

(i)	parama	+	aiśvaryam	=	paramaiśvaryam
	Extreme	+	power	=	supremacy
(ii)	mahā	+	auṣadhiḥ	=	mahauṣadhiḥ
	Strong	+	herb	=	very efficacious medicinal herb
(iii)	tasya	+	audāryam	=	tasyaudāryam
	His	+	generosity	=	his generosity

When **a** or **ā** precedes **ṛ**, **ṛṛ** both letters correspond to **ar**—

(i)	sukha	+	ṛtaḥ	=	sukhārtaḥ
	Joy	+	affected	=	affected by joy
(ii)	pra	+	ṛṇam	=	prārṇam
	Main(pre)	+	debt	=	main debt

These are the characteristics of **vṛddhi** sandhi.

(d) When **i ī**, **u ū**, **ṛ ṝ** and **ḷ** precede a vowel other than the previous one, the former corresponds to **y**, **v**, **r** and **l**, the latter vowel remains the same—

(i)	yadi	+	api	=	yadyapi
	If	+	also	=	even though
(ii)	iti	+	āha	=	ityāh
	Thus	+	said	=	said so
(iii)	madhu	+	ariḥ	=	madhvariḥ
	A demon	+	enemy	=	Vishnu (enemy of Madhu)
(iv)	mātṛ	+	anśaḥ	=	mātranśaḥ
	Mother	+	part	=	mother's part

This is known as **Yaṇ** sandhi.

(e) When **e ai**, **o**, **au** precede a vowel, these change to **ay āy**, **av āv** respectively and the following vowel remains the same—

(i)	ne	+	anam	=	nayanam (eye)
(ii)	nai	+	akaḥ	=	nāyakaḥ (a hero)
(iii)	po	+	anam	=	pavanam (wind)
(iv)	pau	+	akaḥ	=	pāvakaḥ (purifier, fire)

These changes occur in **ayādi** sandhi.

Sometimes, **y** and **v** are dropped also in this sandhi—

(i)	hare	+	iha	=	harayih/hara iha (Vishnu! here)
(ii)	viṣṇo	+	iha	=	viṣṇaviha/viṣṇa iha (Vishnu! here)

(f) When final **e** or **o** is followed by an initial short **a**, the latter vowel merges into the former one and an avagraha takes place instead, it is known as **pūrvarūpa** sandhi;

(i)	hare	+	ava	=	hare'va (protect, O Hari)

(ii) viṣṇo	+	ava	=	viṣṇo'va (protect, O Vishnu)

If the word **go** precedes an **a**, then **a** changes to an avagraha (ऽ) sign by option, the preceding **o** may also change to **av**—

go	+ agram	=	go'gram/gavāgram (chief among cows)

(g) If an **a** of the preposition precedes an **e** or **o**, then **a** merges into that **e** or **o** it is known as **pararūpa** sandhi;

(i) pra	+	ejate	=	prejate (shakes very much)
(ii) upa	+	oṣati	=	upoṣati (burns something nearby)

No Sadhi occurs

(a) Between final **ī**, **ū**, **e** and an initial vowel, if both words indicate the dual number or if the preceding word, in the meaning of **adas** (this) is used in plural number—

(i) harī	+	etau	=	harī etau (these two Haris)
(ii) gange	+	amū	=	gange amū (these two Gangas)
(iii) amī	+	īśāḥ	=	amī īśāḥ (these gods)

(b) With particle of a single vowel, except **ā** in the meaning of 'a little'—

(i) i	+	indraḥ	=	i indraḥ (on Indra)
(ii) u	+	umeśaḥ	=	u umeśaḥ (on Shiva) but
(iii) ā	+	uṣṇam	=	oṣṇam (a little warm)

(c) With an indeclinable ending on O—

Aho	+ apehi	=	aho apehi (o, go away)

(d) with **pluta** or protracted vowels—

ehi kṛṣṇa3 atra gauścarati = come here Krishna, the cow is grazing here.

Vyañjana Sandhi or Coalescence between Final Consonant and Vowel or Consonant—

The final consonant in the preceding word, changes to some other consonant if followed by a vowel or a consonant.

(a) The 1st, 2nd, and 4th consonant of any group changes to the 3rd consonant of that group, if it is succeeded by a sonant vowel or a sonant consonant in the following word—

(i)	samyak	+	āha	=	samyagāh (rightly said)
(ii)	vāk	+	īśaḥ	=	vāgīśaḥ (lord of speech)
(iii)	ṣaṭ	+	ānanaḥ	=	ṣaḍananaḥ (Vishnu)
(iv)	ut	+	deśyam	=	uddeśyam (purpose)

Similarly, 1st, 2nd and 4th consonants of all 5 groups change to 3rd consonant, if followed by a 4th consonant of a group—

(i)	dugh	+	dham	=	dugdham (milk)
(ii)	labh	+	dhaḥ	=	labdhaḥ (begotten)

(b) Consonants of the 5 groups change to a nasal of that group if they precede a nasal—

(i)	sad	+	matiḥ	=	sanmatiḥ (good sense)
(ii)	dik	+	nāgaḥ	=	diṅnāgaḥ (elephant of the direction Or a Buddhist author)

(c) The final m of a word changes to anusvāra if followed by a consonant—

(i) harim	+	vande	=	hariṁvande (obeisance to Hari/ Vishnu)
(ii) satyam	+	vada	=	satyaṁvada (speak the truth)

(d) An anusvāra changes to a 5th nasal consonant of the group of the succeeding consonant—

(i) śaṁ	+	kā	=	śaṅkā (doubt)
(ii) śāṁ	+	taḥ	=	śāntaḥ (at peace)
(iii) aṁ	+	kaḥ	=	aṅkaḥ (mark)

(e) A final anusvāra may change to the nasal of the group of the succeeding consonant optionally, if it belongs to a 'pada' (word)—

(i) tṛṇam	+	carati	=	tṛṇaṁcarati/tṛṇañ carati (eats grass)
(ii) grāmam	+	gacchati	=	grāmaṁgacchati/ grāmam gacchati (goes to the village)

(f) Final consonants of all 5 groups may change to nasal optionally, if followed by a nasal consonant—

(i) dhig	+	mūrkham	=	dhiṅmūrkham/ dhigmūrkham (shame upon the idiot)
(ii) ṣaḍ	+	māsāḥ	=	ṣaṇmāsāḥ/ ṣaḍmāsāḥ (six months)

Exception—

If the consonant is succeeded by a nasal in a preposition, then it will definitely change to a nasal—

(i) tad	+	mātram	=	tanmātram (that much)
(ii) vāg	+	mātram	=	vāṅmātram (only speech)

(g) Final n and m change to anusvāra if succeeded by a s—

(i) yaśān + si = yaśāṁsi (great fame)

(ii) payān + si = payāṁsi (plenty of milk/water)

(h) The final m of pum word changes to dental s with an anusvāra, if it precedes word kokilaḥ—

Pum + kokilaḥ = puṁskokilaḥ (male cukoo)

(I) M of preposition sam changes to dental s with an anusvāra, if it precedes words like karoti, kṛtam etc.—

(i) sam + karoti = saṁskaroti (does well)

(ii) sam + kṛtam = saṁskṛtam (done well)

(j) The final n of a word changes to dental s with an anusvāra, if it precedes dental 1st and 2nd consonants (t, th) and to ś if it precedes 1st and 2nd palatal (c, ch) and to ṣ, if it precedes 1st and 2nd lingual (ṭ, ṭh)—

(i) patan + taruḥ = pataṁstaruḥ (the falling tree)

(ii) kasmin + cit = kasmiṁścit (in something)

(iii) calan + ṭiṭṭibhiḥ = calaṁsṭiṭṭibhiḥ (moving moth)

(k) The n consonant of a pada changes to ṇ, if the pada has r ṛ or ṣ anywhere before n—

(i) rāmena = rāmeṇa (by Rama)

(ii) rāmānām = rāmāṇām (of Ramas)

Change in Dental Consonant—

(a) The final or initial s and any dental consonant change

to ś and a palatal consonant respectively if they conjoin with a ś or a palatal consonant—

(i) nis	+ cayaḥ	=	niścayaḥ (determination)
(ii) sat	+ caritram	=	saccaritram (good character)
(iii) ut	+ cāraṇam	=	uccāraṇam (pronunciation)

Dentals succeeding ś do not change to palatals—

(i) praś	+ naḥ	=	praśnaḥ (question)
(ii) viś	+ naḥ	=	viśnaḥ (luster)

(b) The final or initial s and dental consonant change to ṣ and lingual consonant respectively, if they coalesce with ṣ or a lingual consonant—

(i) tat	+ ṭīkā	=	taṭṭīkā (that commentary)
(ii) duṣ	+ taḥ	=	duṣṭaḥ (wicked)
(iii) kṛṣ	+ naḥ	=	kṛṣṇaḥ (Krishna)

Exception—

The s and dental consonant do not change to ṣ and a lingual if they succeed a final lingual of a pada, except in the case of nām , navati and nagarī words—

(i) ṣaṭ	+ santaḥ	=	ṣaṭsantaḥ (six saints)
(ii) ṣaṭ	+ te	=	ṣaṭte (those six) and
(i) ṣaṭ	+ nām	=	ṣaṇṇām (of six)
(ii) ṣaṭ	+ nagaryaḥ	=	ṣaṇṇagaryaḥ (six cities)

(c) The dental **t** group changes to **l** if it precedes a **l**—

(i) tat + layaḥ = tallayaḥ (his/her destruction)

(ii) vidvān + likhati = vidvaṁ llikhati (the scholar writes)

(d) Consonants of all 5 groups (unaspirated stop), change to the 1st consonant of that particular group, if they are followed by 1st and 2nd consonant—

(i) sad + kāraḥ = satkāraḥ (respect)

(ii) dig + pālaḥ = dikpālaḥ (protector of the direction)

If these consonants come in the end of a word, then they may change to 1st or 3rd consonant of that group—

rāmāt or rāmād

vāk or vāg

(e) Initial h, if preceded by one of the first 4 consonants of any group, changes to the 4th consonant of that group—

(i) vāg + hariḥ = vāggahariḥ (the possessor of speech, Bṛhaspati)

(ii) tad + hitam = taddhitam (his welfare)

(f) Initial ś changes to cch optionally, if preceded by first 4 consonants of any group and if succeeded by a vowel, semi vowel or a h—

(i) tat + śivaḥ = tacchivaḥ/ tacśivaḥ (that Shiva)

(ii) sat + śīlaḥ = sacchīlaḥ/ sacśīlaḥ (good behaviour)

(g) In a word, s changes to ṣ if it is preceded by a vowel, a semi vowel or a guttural of k group—

(i) rāmesu = rāmeṣu (in rāmas)

(ii) pipaṭhisati = pipaṭhiṣati (desires to **read)**

(h) C consonant is inserted between a final short **vowel and** a ch—

(i) śiva + chāyā = śivacchāyā (Shiva's **shadow)**

(ii) sva + chandaḥ = svacchandaḥ (own free will)

(I) C is inserted optionally between a final long vowel and a ch—

Lakśmī + chāyā = lakśmīcchāyā (Lakshmi's **shadow)**

(j) C Must be inserted between a long ā and a ch—

ā + chādayati = ācchādayati (covers)

Visarga Sandhi—

When a certain consonant coalesces with a **vowel or** other consonant, it changes to a short **ḥ** (visarga—:). **When** a visarga coalesces with a vowel, it changes to a **vowel and** when it coalesces with a consonant, it changes to a consonant.

(a) Visarga, if preceded by a short **a**, changes to **o** and the succeeding short **a** becomes an avagrah (ऽ)—

(i) kaḥ + ayam = ko'yam कोऽयम्(who is it)

(ii) bālaḥ + asti = bālo'sti बालोऽस्ति (the child is here)

(iii) nṛpaḥ + avadat = nṛpo'vadat नृपोऽवदत् (the king spoke)

(b) Visarga, if followed by 1st and 2nd consonant, changes to **s** and if followed by 1st and 2nd consonants of palatal group, it changes to a palatal **ś**—

(i) viṣṇuḥ + trāyate = viṣṇustrāyate (Vishnu protects)

(ii) bālaḥ	+	calati	=	bālaścalati (the child walks)
(iii) gajāḥ	+	tiṣṭhanti	=	gajāstiṣṭhanti (elephants are sitting)
(iv) kaḥ	+	cit	=	kaścit (someone)

(c) Visarga changes to **r**, if preceded by a vowel (short or long) except **a, ā** and if it precedes a vowel or 1st, 2nd, 3rd and 5th consonants of any group—

(i) hariḥ	+	avadat	=	hariravadat (Hari spoke)
(ii) pituḥ	+	icchā	=	pituricchā (father's wish)
(iii) guroḥ	+	bhāṣaṇam	=	gurorbhāṣaṇam (teacher's speech)

(d) Visarga when preceded by a short **a**, changes to **o**, if it is succeeded by a 3rd, 4th, 5th consonant or a semi vowel—

(i) **śivaḥ**	+	vandyaḥ	=	śivovandyaḥ (Shiva should be Saluted)
(ii) rāmaḥ	+	vadati	=	rāmo vadati (Ram speaks)
(iii) gajaḥ	+	gacchati	=	gajo gacchati (elephant goes)

(e) Visarga changes to **ś, ṣ, s** optionally, if succeeded by **ś, ṣ, s** respectively—

(i) bālaḥ	+	svapiti	=	bālaḥ svapiti/ bālassvapiti (the child is sleeping)
(ii) hariḥ	+	śete	=	hariḥ śete/hariśśete (Hari Sleep)

(f) Visarga changes to dental **s** if succeeded by words like kāra, pāśa, kalpa etc.—

(i) payaḥ	+	pāśam	=	payaspāśam (whirlpool)
(ii) ayaḥ	+	kāraḥ	=	ayaskāraḥ (ironsmith)
(iii) yaśaḥ	+	kāmyati	=	yaśaskāmyati (desires for Fame)

(g) Visarga changes to **s**, if preceded by **a, ā** and to **ṣ** if preceded by **i, u**—

(i) kaḥ	+	kaḥ	=	kaskaḥ
(ii) bhāḥ	+	karaḥ	=	bhāskaraḥ (the sun)
(iii) sarpiḥ + kuṇḍikā			=	sarpiṣkuṇḍikā (the pitcher of Ghee)

(h) Visarga in **namaḥ** word optionally and **puraḥ** word compulsorily, changes to dental **s,** if succeeded by word **karoti**—

(i) namaḥ	+	karoti	=	namaḥ karoti/ namaskaroti (greets)
(ii) puraḥ	+	karoti	=	puraskaroti (puts forward)

(I) Visarga in **tiraḥ** word changes to dental **s,** if it precedes a **k, kh** in the latter word—

(i) tiraḥ	+	karoti	=	tiraskaroti (hides or scorns)
(ii) tiraḥ	+	kṛtam	=	tiraskṛtam (hidden)

(j) If repetitive words indicating **dvi, tri** etc, having visarga are succeeded by **k, kh** or **p, ph,** visarga changes to **s** optionally—

(i) dviḥ	+	karoti	=	dviḥ karoti/ dviskaroti (does twice)

(ii)	catuḥ	+	paṭhati	=	catuḥ paṭhati/ catuspaṭhati (reads four times)

(k) Visarga, when preceded by an **ā** is dropped compulsorily, if it is succeeded by a soft 3rd, 4th, 5th consonant—

(i)	devāḥ	+	namyāḥ	=	devā namyāḥ (gods should be Saluted)
(ii)	narāḥ	+	gacchanti	=	narā gacchanti (men are going)

(l) Visarga when preceded by an **a** or **ā,** is dropped optionally, if it is succeeded by a vowel—

(i)	devāḥ	+	āgacchanti	=	devā āgacchanti/ devāḥ āgacchnti (gods are coming)
(ii)	sutaḥ	+	āgacchati	=	suta āgacchati/ sutaḥ āgacchati (son is coming)

(m) Visarga, succeeded by an i changes to **y** optionally—

Devāḥ	+	iha		devāyiha/devāiha

(n) Visarga is dropped and the preceding vowel becomes long, if it precedes **r**—

(i)	punaḥ	+	ramate	punā ramate (sports again)
(ii)	hariḥ	+	ramyaḥ	harī ramyaḥ (Hari is graceful)

(o) Visarga in words like **saḥ, eṣaḥ,** is dropped if it is succeeded by a consonant—

(i)	saḥ	+	gacchati	=	sa gacchati (he goes)
(ii)	eṣaḥ	+	viṣṇuḥ	=	eṣa viṣṇuḥ (this Vishnu)

Consonant changing to Visarga—

(a) Final **s** of a word changes to visarga—

(i) rāmas = rāmaḥ (Ram)

(ii) kṛṣṇas = kṛṣṇaḥ (Krishna)

(b) Final **s** of a word changes to visarga if succeeded by a hard consonant—

Bālakas	+	paṭhati	=	bālakaḥ paṭhati (the child reads)

(c) **N** of word **ahan** changes to **o** if succeeded by words like **rūpa, rātri** etc—

(i) ahan	+	rātraḥ	=	aho rātraḥ (day and night)
(ii) ahan	+	rūpam	=	aho rūpam (the form of the day)

(d) N of **ahan** changes to **r,** if it is succeeded by word **ahaḥ**—

Ahan	+	ahaḥ	=	aharahaḥ (day by day)

(e) At times in poetry, a visarga is dropped if a vowel follows it and then it takes a **svara sandhi**—

saiṣa dāśarathī rāmaḥ, saiṣa rājā yudhiṣṭhiraḥ.

III.2

Phonology in Manipuri

Manipuri language is found in use in two scripts; Meitei Mayek (Original Manipuri script) and Bengali script. Until the end of the 17th century, Manipuri literature was written in original Manipuri. The Royal Chronicles'Cheitharol Kumbaba' were written in this script only. Later literature on varied subjects like mythology, geography, history was written in original Manipuri. Since 18th century, after religious conversion, Bengali script was adopted for writing and gradually several loan words from Sanskrit, Bengali and Hindi came in use in this language. Manipuri linguists have acknowledged 6 vowels, 6 diphthongs, 24 consonants and 2 tones.

Original Manipuri Alphabet as given below—

MEITEI MAYEK MAPEE
(Manipuri Script)

ꯀ	ꯁ	ꯂ	ꯃ	ꯄ	ꯅ
kok	səm	lay	mit	pa	na
k	s	l	m	p	n
ꯆ	ꯇ	ꯈ	ꯉ	ꯊ	ꯋ
cil	til	khəw	ŋəw	thəw	way
ch	t	kh	ŋ	th	w
ꯌ	ꯍ	ꯎ	ꯏ	ꯐ	ꯑ
yaŋ	huk	un	i	phəm	ətiya
y	h	u	i	p^h	ə

Borrowed Sounds (found in loan words)

ꯒ	ꯘ	ꯕ	ꯚ
g	gh	b	bh
ꯖ	ꯓ	ꯗ	ꯙ
j	jh	d	dh
ꯔ			
r			

Close Consonants (Occurred finally)

ꯛ	ꯜ	ꯝ	ꯞ	ꯟ	ꯠ
k	l	m	p	n	t
ꯡ					
ŋ					

Vowels and Consonants as shown in Modern Manipuri (Bengali):

Vowels—

অ	a	আ	ā	ই	i	এ	e
ও	o	উ	u				

Semi vowels— য (y) and ৱ (v) are semi- vowels which are found in this language. Diphthongs used in Manipuri by combining the vowels and semi-vowels are—

অয	ay	আয	āy	উয	uy
ওয	oy	অৱ	aw	আৱ	āw

Consonants—

ক	K	খ	kh	গ	g	ঘ	gh
ঙ	ṅ	চ	c	জ	j	ঝ	jh
ত	t	থ	th	দ	d	ধ	dh
ন	n	প	P	ফ	ph	ব	b
ভ	bh	ম	m	য	y	র	r
ল	l	ৱ	v	স	s	হ	h

Out of these bh dh gh jh are supposed to have been borrowed from other languages, hence their use is restricted and found only in loan words. Even use of g d b j is not found in old Manipuri script, instead k t p c are used. (Grierson, Linguistic Survey of India, vol.3, pg. 24)

Articulatory System of Vowels— The articulatory system of vowels can be seen from the chart given below—

	Front	*Central*	*Back*
High (close)	i		u
Mid (half close, half open)	e	a	o
Low(close)		ā	

This can be further explained—

i is high, front, unrounded vowel.

e is mid, front, unrounded vowel.

a is mid, central, unrounded vowel.

ā is low, central, unrounded vowel.

u is high, back rounded vowel.

O is mid, back rounded vowel.

Presence of Vowels in a Word— In Manipuri language, vowels can be used at the initial, in the middle or in the end of the word. The examples are given below—

1. Initial use—

abok	—	grandmother,	aṅgā'ṅ	—	child
isiṅ	—	water,	āda	—	there
ok	—	pig,	ucek	—	bird,
ensāṅ	—	curry			

However use of 'ā' and 'e' is not found in common.

2. Medial use— All the vowels can be used in the middle of a word , for example—

yum	—	house	kāṅ	—	mosquito
ceṅ	—	rice	lik	—	necklace

cāk	—	food (cooked rice)	tan	—	bread
pot	—	things (load)	thum	—	salt

3. **Final use—** A vowel can be seen in the end of a word also in Manipuri language—

sanā	—	gold	siba	—	die
yū	—	liquor	tumba	—	sleep
tāmo	—	elder brother	motpa	—	dirty
camprā	—	lemon	makhā	—	down
ice	—	elder sister			

Use of Diphthong sound— We find many words having diphthong sound in Manipuri language—

may	—	fire	koy	—	beard
lay	—	flower	lāy	—	god or picture
makhoy	—	they	khāw	—	bag
huy	—	dog	māy	—	face

Scholars like Bhat and Ningomba (Manipuri Grammar, pg. 21) do not consider such words as having diphthong sounds, since in their view, semi vowels are actually consonants.

Articulatory System of Diphthongs—

	Front	*Centre*	*Back*
Close		ui	
		Oi	
Half close	ai		au
	āy		āu
Half open			

Articulatory System of Consonants—

	Velar		*Palatal*		*Alveolar*		*Bilabial*		*Glottal*	
	vl.	vd.	vl.	vd.	vl.	vd.	vl.	vd.	vl.	vd.
unaspirated	k	g	c	j	t	d	p	b		

STOPS	**aspirated**	kh gh	jh	th dh	ph bh	
	Fricatives		s			h
	Nasals	ṅ		n	m	
	Lateral				l	
	Trill				r	
	Semi-vowels		y		w	

Presence of Consonants in a Word—

In Manipuri, all consonant phonemes are not found in the initial, not all in the middle and not in the end position. Consonants like t th k kh c j p ph m ṅ s h w and y take initial position generally;

kātin	—	scissors	kay	—	tiger
khudeṅ	—	a large plate	khupāṅ	—	palm
tandan	—	firefly	tāmo	—	elder brother
tharo	—	lily	thāsi	—	month
camprā	—	lemon	cākhum	—	kitchen
mit	—	eye	nā	—	ear
numit	—	sun	sam	—	hair
sā	—	meat	haujik	—	now
huy	—	dog	jagoy	—	dance
pāra	—	lesson	pūba	—	to carry
phamuṅ	—	bed	phi	—	cloth
mī	—	people	ṅgā	—	fish
ṅgamba	—	possible	lasiṅ	—	cotton
lā	—	banana leaf	wāri	—	story
wā	—	bamboo	yāri	—	jaw (gum)
yoṅ	—	monkey			

Loan words having consonants initially —

There are other consonants which are seen in loan words in initial position, they are—b bh d dh jh g gh and r. The examples are as follows;

bāmon	—	Brahmin (one of the four castes)	borā	—	bag (jute sack)
bhāri	—	heavy	Bhut	—	ghost
dukān	—	shop	dolāy	—	palanquin
dhon/l	—	drum	dhama	—	religion
govinda	—	lord Krishna	gāri	—	vehicle
ghari	—	wrist watch	raṅg	—	colour
rās	—	a kind of dance			

Medial Position—

Almost all consonants except a few can occur in the medial position in a word—

laykāy	—	locality	laykhom	—	mud
atanba	—	lazy	atomba	—	younger
macu	—	colour	mamal	—	cost
lasiṅ	—	cotton	marāṅgoy	—	a fruit
awāṅgba	—	height	aṅgāṅ	—	child
khudeṅ	—	a large plate	khuji	—	finger
mathak	—	above	mamāy	—	face
mayāy	—	in the middle	manam	—	smell
lamhui	—	fox			

Aspirated voiced consonants like bh dh gh jh are not found in the medial position.

Final Position— The consonants which occur in the end of a word, are very few and they are k t p m n l ṅ y w . The examples are—

laybāk	—	soil	layrik	—	book
pot	—	thing	thoṅ	—	door
siṅ	—	ginger	hay	—	fruit

noṅyāy	—	midnight	matam	—	time
maman/l	—	cost	pāt	—	lake (pond)
aṅgāṅ	—	child	khāw	—	bag
pāw	—	news			

Consonants like r s c and h are not found in the final use in Manipuri words, but they do occur in loan words, for example—

kār	—	car	acār	—	pickle
pulis	—	police	bas	—	bus

Common Consonant Clusters— Like Tibeto- Burman languages, consonant clusters are found at the initial and medial level. Most common clusters are kw, ky, dw, tr, pr at the initial level and pw, kr, khr, gr, etc at the medial level—

Initial cluster—

kwā	—	betel nut	kwāk	—	crow
khwāṅ	—	waist	klās	—	class
swāyda	—	here	adwāyda	—	there
tren	—	train			

Medial Cluster—

ṅgakrā	—	a kind of fish	camprā	—	lemon
hayjrāṅ	—	kitchen knife	maṅgrā	—	sweet potato
mawpwā	—	her younger brother	lāysram	—	a surname

Consonant Sequence— There are a number of consonants like p t k ph th kh m n l ṅ s h y, which are used immediately after a consonant, that is p t k m n ṅ. This sequence occurs beyond a syllable, we can understand by the examples given below—

With **p** as first consonant—

kappa	—	cry	akāpmal	—	fees for injection
tappa	—	slow	kapsinba	—	cry continuously

lepkaṅ	— a dry tree	tapsinba	— to be added
kupyān	— cut into small pieces		

With **t** as first consonant—

patpa	— rot	katpa	— offer
khutcā	— of eating	litnaba	— to wear
khutsā	— fingers	phattaba	— bad
khutyāy	— middle finger		

With **k** as first consonant—

sakpa	— to sing	hākpa	— to kill
pokpa	— to give birth	hakcāṅ	— body
pokkhāyba	— to burst	liklā	— dew
pikmanba	— very small		

With **m** as first consonant—

lamkoyba	— travel,	lambi	— road/way,
tampāk	— valley,	lamjel	— race
lamjā	— orphan,	samcet	— comb,
samkak	— hair style		

With **n** as first consonant—

kāntha	— quilt,	lānpham	— battlefield,
tandan	— firefly,	tanba	— lazy
yensāṅ	— curry,	laṅgay	— treasure,
sinmi	— worker	tamna	— slowly
hentāk	— fermented fish	tankhāy	— half

With **ṅ** as first consonant—

thāṅtup	— a kind of plant	leṅbān	— shoulder
kāṅhan	— mosquito net	noṅsā	— licn
yoṅcāk	— a kind of vegetable	kāṅbu	— group
laṅyāy	— a kind of thread	nuṅdāṅ	— night
kāṅṅgaw	— fried vegetable		

With **l** as first consonant—

mālhai	—	plum	kolhiṅ	—	rust

Tone— There are two types of tones in Manipuri language— mid and low. Phoneme in low tone takes longer duration than in mid tone. Mid tone is shown without any mark and low is shown with a mark ('). This distinction is seen more clearly in Chinese and Burmese languages as compared to Manipuri language. This tonal distinction is applied in places where it is linguistically required, below are given some examples—

Mid			**low**		
mi	—	people	mì	—	spider
khoṅ	—	leg	khòṅ	—	stream
lā	—	basket	là	—	banana leaf
lem	—	left out	lèm	—	grave
thi	—	ugly	thì	—	search
i	—	blood	ì	—	thatch
siṅ	—	ginger	sìṅ	—	firewood

Phonological Changes— Phonological Changes occur while coalescing words or morphemes. These changes are seen in the final position of the first word and in the initial position of the latter word; that could be a vowel or a consonant. This change also occurs in the form of deletion of the vowel or consonant.

Change in Vowel— In the final syllable of the first word a vowel changes; ā to a, e to a and o to u. The final consonant is deleted and the initial voiceless stop changes to voiced stop; the examples are—

cāk (cooked rice)	+ kā (blackened)	= cagā (burnt rice)
khut (hand)	+ cin (tip)	= khujin (nail)
thā (chest)	+ pāk (broad)	= thabāk (chest)

Sometimes there is no change in the vowel, the end consonant is deleted and the lateral (l) changes to trill (r)—

yen (hen)	+	lum (egg)	=	yerum (egg)

Change in Consonant— Change occurs to both sounds; end and first of both words by mutual influence. Voiceless stops change to voiced if they are preceded by a nasal sound in the previous word; nasal m changes to ṅ and n to m, by being influenced by the following sound. The examples are—

kom (pit)	+	kut (depressed)	=	koṅgut (a pit)
san (cow)	+	pān (barrier)	=	sambān (fence)
san (cow)	+	khom (milk)	=	saṅgom (milk)
yen (hen)	+	kon (shed)	=	yeṅgon (poultry)

If n is followed by l or h, then n changes to l; for example—

Root						Suffix
tan (lazy)	+	le			=	talle (being lazy)
cen (run)	+	le			=	celle (ran)
yon (sell)	+	han (cause)	+	le	=	yolhalle (made him sell)

Initial aspirated stop of the root changes to unaspirated stop of the same group, if it follows a root having an unaspirated stop; for example—

thak (drink)	+	thok (completely)	+	le	=	thaktokle (drank completely)
hāt (kill)	+	thok (completely)	+	le	=	hāttokle (has killed)
khak (stop)	+	khat (begin)	+	le	=	khakkatle (began to stop)
hāp (add)	+	khat (begin)	+	le	=	hāpkatle (added up)

Lateral l of the succeeding suffix changes to the same consonant if it is preceded by p m ṅ and w; for example—

tum (sleep)	+	le	=	tumme (slept)
caṅ (enter)	+	le	=	caṅṅge (entered)
law (take)	+	le	=	lawwe (took)

kup (cover) + le = kuppe (covered)

Deletion of Vowel— Vowel ā is deleted when it precedes an a—

cā (hundred) + ani (two) = cani (two hundred)

cā (hundred) + ahum (three) = cahum (three hundred)

Sometimes the succeeding a is deleted if there is an ā in the preceding word—

tarā (ten) + amāthoy (one exceed) = tarāmāthoy (eleven)

cā (hundred) + amā (one) = camā (one hundred)

Deletion of Consonant— the preceding **t** is deleted if it is followed by a **t** and the second **t** changes to voiced **d**—

khut (hand) + top (add) = khudop (ring)

Sometimes the end consonant **k** is deleted, the latter initial lateral **l** changes to **r**—

thok (come) + lakpa (out) = thorakpa (come out)

Deletion of Nasal Sound— The initial nasal sound is deleted when it follows nasal—

im (house) + nuṅ (inside) = imuṅ (inside the house)

The end nasal sound is deleted and preceding o changes to u ,if it is followed by a nasal sound in the second word—

khoṅ (leg) + niṅ (back) = khuniṅ (heel)

Conclusion

Similarities—

(1) Sanskrit and Manipuri, both languages have main vowels in their alphabets— a, i, u, e, o. Besides old Manipuri script, there is Bengali script also which is effectively in use in Manipuri language. Therefore, there are 11 vowels in Bengali script in use, which is 3 vowels short of Sanskrit vowels; ṛ, ṛṛ and lṛ.

(2) There are 31 consonants which are used in Manipuri language, although voiced stops are supposed to be

borrowed from Sanskrit and other languages. There are 33 consonants in Sanskrit.

(3) The phonetic system of both languages is quite similar.

(4) All vowels can be used initially, medially and in the end of a word in both languages.

(5) Conjunct consonants are very much in use in Sanskrit and Manipuri both.

(6) Sanskrit and Manipuri both have tones, though in Sanskrit it is found prevalent in Vedic literature.

(7) In euphony, initial and final changes occur in both languages; for example—

Dental n changes to l if followed by a l—

Sanskrit— vidvān + likhati		=	vidvāṁllikhati (scholar writes) Here the nasal sound is retained.
Manipuri— tan	+ le	=	talle (feeling lazy/ uninterested)

Dissimilarities—

Sanskrit and Manipuri both languages belong to two different language groups, hence there is a difference in the number of vowels and consonants.

1. Sanskrit has 13 vowels including 4 diphthongs, where as old Manipuri script has 12 vowels including 6 diphthongs. The diphthongs in Sanskrit are e ai o au, the diphthongs in Manipuri are ay āy oy uy aw āw.
2. There is no long ī ū ṛ ṛṛ and lṛ in Manipuri.
3. There are 33 consonants in Sanskrit and 24 in Manipuri. In old Manipuri the use of ch ṣ ñ and ś is not seen. Consonants k t p c were in use instead of g d b j in old Manipuri.
4. The articulatory system is different in both languages; w is bilabial in Manipuri where as it is both bilabial as

well as dental in Sanskrit.

5. In Sanskrit under certain condition, the nasal sound may change to an anusvāra or anunāsika, these sounds and signs are common in use.
6. The final s or r in a word changes to a visarga in Sanskrit.
7. **A** changes to an avagraha (ऽ) if followed by an **e** or **o** in Sanskrit.
8. The svarita tone which is a combination of both udātta (acute) and anudātta (grave) is also used in Sanskrit which we do not see in Manipuri.
9. The vowel in the final syllable, in Manipuri becomes short in coalescing with another word—

Cāk	kā	=	cagā
Rice	blackened	=	burnt rice

10. While coalescing, the final consonant of the previous word is dropped—

khut	top	=	khudop
Hand	add	=	ring

11. A lateral sound changes to trill and the final consonant is dropped—

Thok	lakpa	=	thorakpa
Come	out	=	come out

12. In Manipuri final ā is dropped when it precedes an a—

Cā	ani	=	cani
Hundred	two	=	two hundred

13. In Sanskrit in such situation both vowels become long (dīrgha)—

Vidyā	arthī	=	vidyārthī
Learning	desirous	=	student

The Pūrvarūpa and Pararūpa Sandhis are an essential ingredient of Sanskrit language.

IV.1

Tense and Mood in Sanskrit

Tense is an inflectional part of the verb which indicates time of action taking place. Tense derives from the Greek word for 'time' which originates from Latin word 'tempus'. The category of time indicates the relation of verb with location of time. According to Hockitt, "Tenses typically show different locations of an event in time." (A Course in Modern Linguistics, New York, Macmillan, 1958 pg.237) The grammatical contrasts of time relations have been categorized as 'past, present and future'. Tense signifies the location of time in a sentence— mother cooks (in present) and mother cooked (in past) but when the sentence is 'mother is cooking', it is dealt by 'aspect' not by 'tense'. Therefore aspect indicates the (internal) temporal structure of an action; how it is taking place— whether it is completed or will be completed or is it still continuing. Besides tense and aspect, there is one more inflectional part that is 'mood' or 'mode'. Mood shows the manner in which an action or a situation is stated. Mood connotes the mental state which is indicative of the state of verb.

Tenses in Sanskrit— There are five tenses and five moods in Sanskrit which are indicated by Lakāras, they are— **laṭ, liṭ, luṭ, lṛṭ, leṭ, loṭ, laṅ, liṅ, luṅ** and **lṛṅ**. These are placed by Pāṇini in the phonological order. Out of these each **'la'** is left, rest of the letters are omitted, hence known as lakāras. Leṭ lakāra is an archaic lakāra, it has occurred in Vedic literature.

Present is indicated by 'laṭ' lakāra. Future is shown by two lakāras— lṛṭ (simple future) and luṭ (periphrastic future) and past is indicated by three lakāras— laṅ, liṭ and luṅ. Laṅ lakāra indicates the Imperfect Past, liṭ lakāra is used for Perfect Past and luṅ lakāra indicates the Aorist— the past as well as the recent time in which the action has taken place. In earlier times when Sanskrit was a common language of people, this time differentiation of Lakāras denoting divisions of Past and Future Tense was strictly followed, later on scholars stopped observing these strict rules. The remaining lakāras are not indicative of time but of mood. Loṭ lakāra indicates Imperative Mood, Liṅ Lakāra is divided into two— Vidhiliṅ (the Optative or Potential Mood) and Āśīrliṅ (the Benedictive or Proactive Mood). Vidhiliṅ or Potential Mood is used to indicate ethics, to command a subordinate etc. Āśīrliṅ or the Benedictive is used to express wish or give blessings. Loṭ lakāra or the Imperative Mood may also be used for command and blessing. Lṛṅ lakāra is a Conditional Mood which indicates past incomplete reality.

In Sanskrit grammar there is no provision for Aspect— the internal temporal constituency of the structure. The action taking place at the present moment or progressing, is dealt by Laṭ Lakāra only; adverb may be added for showing the progress of action. Similarly, Laṭ Lakāra also indicates a situation where action has taken place moments before present or going to take place moments after present.

Languages like Latin and Greek have more developed tenses and moods than Sanskrit but some tenses and moods are peculiar in Sanskrit. Below is given the table to show the 10 tenses and moods:

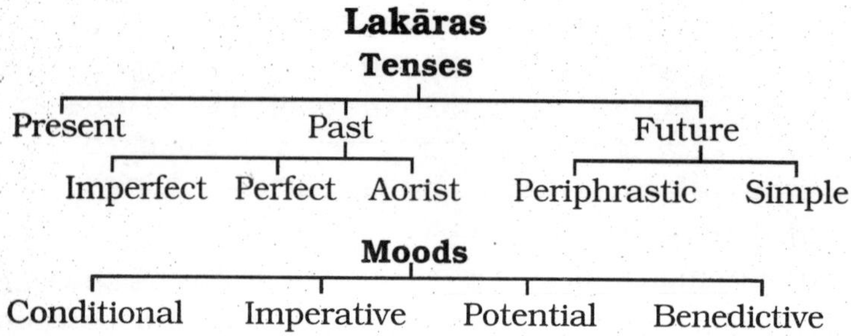

Present Tense— The Present Tense denotes an action taking place or signifying an existing fact, in the present time. In fact, the present indicates progressive, imperfect or yet to be completed action, such as;

1.

etāstapasvikanyakāḥ			*ita*	*evābhivartate*
These	ascetic	girls	here	only coming
pro	adj	noun	adv.	expres. action pres.

These ascetic girls are coming in this dircction only.

2.

mātā	*yācakāya*	*vastram*	*dadāti.*
Mother	begger	clothe	give
nom. case	noun dat.	accus sing no.	verb
sing no.	sing no.		3rd pers.
			pres.

Mother gives clothe to the begger.

In Sanskrit there is no separate Lakāra or Tense to signify the present progressive state, this situation is expressed by the same Laṭ Lakāra—

1.

adhunā	*sa*	*pātālaloke*	*vasati.*
Now conj	he pro.	Patalaloka noun	live verb
	nomi. case	loc. case	pres. tense
			sing. no.

At present he is dwelling in the Patalaloka.

2.

katham	*ito'pi*	*mām*	*anusarati.* (śaku. canto i.)
Why adv.	Here adv.	I pro. accu.	follow verb
	too expr.	case sing.no.	pres. 3rd pers.
			sing. no.

Why it is following me here too.

To put stress to the present situation, an adverb is added in a sentence; **adhunā**, **samprati** etc. The all time true situation indicated by Present Indefinite as described by Bain (Grammar, pg.185) and the law of nature, the permanent thing etc. are expressed in Sanskrit by Laṭ Lakāra—

1. *himālayāt* — The Himalayas noun abl. case sing. no. | *gaṅgā* — Ganga noun nomi. case | *prabhavati.* — originate verb pres. tense, sing. no.

   The Ganga originates from the Himalayas.

2. *vidyā* — Knowledge noun nom. case | *dadāti* — give verb pres. tense 3rd pers. sing. no. | *vinayam.* — humility noun accus. case sing. no.

   Knowledge brings humility.

Laṭ Lakāra also denotes the past which has just gone by and the future, just next to it, for example— on asking 'when did you come' the person replies—

ayam — This pro. | *āgacchāmi.* — arrive verb pres. tense 1st pers. sing. no.

I have just arrived.

Or on asking' when will you go' the person replies—

eṣa — This pro. | *gacchāmi.* — go verb pres. tense. Ist pers.sing. no.

I will go just now.

In a compound sentence, the subordinate sentence signifying future, generally takes present tense .Words like **'yāvat, purā'** etc. are used to express future, for example—

1. *pustakam* — Book noun accus. case sing. no. | *paṭhitavyam* — read participle | *tvayā* — you pro. inst. sing no.

   yāvat — till adv. | *ahamāgacchāmi.* — I pron. | come. verb pres. 1st pers.sing. no.

   You should read the book till I come.

The Present Tense is also used to indicate the conditional situations—

yo	*gurūn*	*śuśrūṣati*
Who rel. pro. nom.	elder noun accu. case plu. no.	serve verb pres. tense sing.
sa	*sukham*	*prāpnoti.*
He pro.nom.	case happiness noun neu. gen.	attain verb pres. tense sing.

He who serves elders, attains happiness.

While narrating a story, sometimes Present Tense is used—

kasminścit	*vane*	*ekaḥ*
Some inde. pro.	forest noun loc. case sing.	one numeral

siṁhaḥ	*nivasati.*
lion noun nom.case	live verb pres.tense 3rd pers.sing.

A lion used to live in a forest.

Sometimes in narration word **'sma'** is added to the verb in Present to indicate the Imperfect Past—

kasminścit	*kūpe*	*gangadatto*	*nāma*
Some inde. pro.	well noun loc. case	Gangadatta Noun	name noun

maṇḍūkarājaḥ	*prativasati*	*sma.*
Frog noun nom. case	live verb pres. tense 3rd pers. sing. no.	particle

A frog named Gangadatta used to live in a forest.

Sometimes a desire in future is conveyed in Present Tense with interrogatives—

kim	*karomi*	*kva*	*gacchāmi.*
What interr. pro.	do verb pres. tense 1st pers.	where inter. pro.	go verb pres. 1st pers. sing. no.

What shall I do, where shall I go?

Or

kim	*gacchāmi*	*dillīm.*
What inter. pro.	go verb pres. tense 1st pers. sing. no.	Delhi noun accus. case

Should I go to Delhi.

Past Tense— In Sanskrit there are three types of Past Tenses— Imperfect, Perfect and Aorist. When Sanskrit was more prevalent in society, all these three past tenses were used to signify different time and condition, but in the later period people started using these tenses promiscuously.

The Imperfect Past— The Imperfect Past Tense is denoted by **Laṅ Lakāra**, it indicates past action which is not performed today and which is done previous to the current day—

1\.

saḥ	*hyaḥ*	*bhojanam*	*akarot.*
He pro. nomi. case	yesterday adv.	food noun accus. case	eat verb imp. past 3rd pers. sing. no.

He had his food yesterday.

2\.

evam	*bile*	*praviśantam*	*kṛṣṇasarpam*
Thus adv.	hole noun loc.case	enter verb participle	black serpant adj. noun accu.

apaśyat.
see verb
imp. past
3rd pers. sing.

Thus he saw a black serpant entering the hole.

The Imperfect is also used to ask a question regarding recent time—

agacchat	*kim*	*sa*	*gṛham?*
Go verb imp. past 3rd pers. sing.no.	what inter. pro.	he pers. pro. nom.	house noun accus. case

Has he gone home?

The answer is 'agacchat' (gone).

To indicate the Imperative (negative), particle **mā** is used along with **sma** and the augment **a** is dropped—

1. *mā sma* — *karot.*
   Imper.neg. particle — do verb imp. past 2nd pers. sing. no.

   Do not do.

2. *mā* — *devadatta* — *sma* — *harat.*
   Imper. neg. par. — Devadatta noun voc. case — particle — abduct verb imp. past 2nd pers. sing. no.

   O Devadatta, do not abduct.

The Imperfect Past is also used in narration of incidents and optionally in place of Perfect— iti ha avadat or uvāca (thus said), śaśvadapaṭhat or papāṭha (read).

The Perfect Past— In Sanskrit, the Perfect Past is indicated by Liṭ Lakāra. It signifies the action done the previous day or before that and which is not witnessed by the speaker. The Perfect is commonly used while narrating past events. In this tense the verb is duplicated—

Atha	*siṁhe*	*gate*	*kaścit*
Thus particle	lion loc. case	go verb past part.loc.case	a inde. pro.

vyāghraḥ	*samāyayau.*
tiger noun nomi.case	come verb perf. past 3rd pers. sing. no.

After the lion left, a tiger came there.

In narration, the Perfect Past is used by the 1st person only when the speaker has been in an unconscious state of mind. In **Dasakumaracaritam** in narration the Perfect

Past has not been used when the adventurers describe their own experiences, the same observation is with **Kathasaritsagara**. There are one or two instances in Sanskrit literature where 1st person uses Perfect Past but that seems more to conceal the truth as we observe in the following dialogue— kaliṅgeṣvavātsīḥ. (did you not dwell in the Kalinga).

The answer is— nāham kaliṅgān jagāma. (I did not go to Kalinga, implying forget about my stay there.)

The Aorist— The Aorist known as Luṅ Lakāra is used for past in general sense, it could be both recent or historical. It may even denote action done during the present day. According to Dr. R.G.Bhandarakar, "it is similar to the English Present Perfect." (Second Book of Sanskrit, pg. 154), for example—

abhūt	*vṛṣṭiḥ*	*adya.*
Happen verb aorist	rain noun	today
3rd pers. sing. no.	nomi. case	adverb

It rained today.

The Aorist is also used to imply the continuity of action—

brāhmaṇebhyo	*yāvat*	*jīvam*
The Brahmanas	till adv.	life noun
noun dat.plu.no.		accus.
annam	*adāt.*	
food	give	
noun accu.	verb aor.3rd pers. sing. no.	

He gave food to the Brahmanas for as long as he lived.

With the use of **purā** 'formerly', not joined with **sma**; all three past tenses and the present may be used—

purā	*ayodhyānagaryām*	*daśaratho*
Earlier	Ayodhya noun loc.	Dasaratha
adv.	case	noun

nāma	*nṛpatiḥ*
name adverbial noun	king noun sing. no.

vasati/	*avasat/*	*uvāsa/*	*avātsīt.*
live verb pres./	imper.past/	perf. past/	aorist.

Earlier a king named Daśaratha lived in Ayodhya.

But if **sma** is joined with **purā**, then only present is used—

Nṛtyati	*sma*	*purā.*
Dance verb pres. sing. no.	particle	earlier.

She used to dance earlier.

The augment **a** is generally cut-off from the Aorist with the use of **mā** or **mā sma**—

mā sma	*pratīpam*	*gamaḥ.*
Neg. particle	against adverb	go verb aorist 2nd pers. sing. no.

Do not act against him. (śākuntalam).

Sometimes this **a** is retained also as in—

mā	*niṣāda*	*pratiṣṭhām*	*tvam*
Neg. part.	hunter noun vocat.case	thrive noun accu.	you pron. sing. no.

agamaḥ...
attain verb aorist.

O hunter, may you not thrive.......

Participles **kta** and **ktavatu** are also used to indicate past— the Aorist;

1.

eṣa	*mṛgo*	*viprakṛṣṭāntaraḥ*
This demo. pron.	deer noun nomi. case	far reaching noun

saṁvṛttaḥ.
become verb with
kta participle sing. no.

This deer has become quite far reaching. (Śākuntalam)

2.

anaṣūye,	*gatavatī*	*vām*
Anasuya noun voc.	depart verb with participle ktavatu	you poss. pron.

sahadharmcāriṇī.
companion noun
sing. no.

Anasuya, your companion has departed.

Sometimes the use of **kta** also indicates the present—

suptaḥ	*bālakaḥ.*
Sleep verb with kta part.	child noun sing. no.

The child is asleep or sleeping.

Participle **kta** is also used in Passive Voice—**bhāvavācya** and **karmavācya**—

bālakena	*pustakam*	*paṭhitam.*
Child noun instr. karmavācya	book noun nom. case	read verb with kta participle.

The book was read by the boy. Or

śiśunā	*ruditam.*
Child noun instr.case—bhāvavācya	cry verb with **kta** participle.

Crying was done by the child.

Participle **ktavatu** is used in Active Voice—

viśvam	*kṛtavān*	*viṣṇuḥ.*
World noun accu.	create verb with ktavatu parti. sing. no.	Visnu noun nom. case.

Visnu created the world.

Future Tense— In Sanskrit two types of Future have been

discussed—1. Periphrastic Future— it talks about only those events which are going to occur after today 2. Simple Future—it deals with future in general. The difference between the two is the same what is between Imperfect and Perfect Past.

1. Periphrastic Future— Periphrastic Future is known as **luṭ lakāra** in Sanskrit, it denotes Future which is going to occur any other day in future but today, for example—

1\.

śvaḥ	*gantāsmi.*
Tomorrow adverb	go verb peri. future 1st pers. sing. no.

I shall go tomorrow.

2\.

pañcaśeiḥ	*ahobhiḥ*	*vayameva*	*tatra*
Five six adj.	day noun inst. case plu. no.	we only pers. pro. nomi.case	there adverb

gantāraḥ.(Mud.5)
go verb peri.future
1st pers
plu. no.

In five- six days we ourselves will go there.

In Sanskrit the Periphrastic Future is treated as a remote future, it is less frequently used as compared with the Simple Future.

2. Simple Future— This Future, known as **lṛṭ lakāra** denotes future in general; indefinite and recent future.It can signify action taking place today also and future in progress—

1\.

yāsyati	*adya*	*śakuntaleti......* *(Śākuntalam.IV)*
Go verb simp. future 3rd pers. sing. no.	today adv.	Sakuntala noun this nomi. indecl.

This that Sakuntala will leave today....

2.

nāham	*tava*	*mūrkhasya*	*upadeśam*
Not I	you	idiot	lecture
neg. part.	pers. pro.	adj. gen.	noun accus.
pers.pro. nomi.	geni.		sing.no.

api	*dāsyāmi. (pañc)*
also	give verb simp. future.
parti.	1st per.sing. no.

I will not even lecture you idiot.

3.

yāvat	*jīvam*	*adhyāpayiṣyati.*
Till adverb	life noun	teach verb simp. future
	accus. case	3rd per. sing. no.

He will teach throughout his life.

The Simple Future also denotes desire, intention, purpose etc.—

saḥ	*paṭhiṣyati*	*iti*	*gṛham*	*gacchati.*
He	study	hence	home	go
pers.	verb simp.	part.	noun accus.	verb pres. 3rd
pro.	future		sing.no.	pers. sing.no.

He goes home because he will study.

Simple Future is also used to indicate near future or in the close proximity of the Future optionally as in the reply of a question below—

kadā	*lekhiṣyasi*
When adverb	write verb simp. future
	2nd pers. sing. no.

When will you write.

eṣa	*likhāmi/*	*lekhiṣyāmi.*
This	write verb pres. tense/	simple future 1st
pron.		pers. sing. no.

I am just writing or I will just write.

Sometimes Simple Future is also used in the Imperative manner as courtesy—

paścāt	*saram*	*prati*	*gamiṣyasi.(Vikra.4)*
Later adverb	lake noun accu.	particle	go verb simp. future 2nd pers. sing. no.

Later you will go to the lake. And

tadā	*mama*	*pāśān*	*chhetsyasi.* (Hitop.1)
Then adverb	I poss. pro. sing. no.	rope noun accus. plu. no.	cut verb simp. future 2nd pers. sing. no.

Then cut my ropes.

When hope is implied in a conditional form in a sentence, then the Aorist, the Present and the Simple Future can be used optionally in both the sentences—

devaḥ	*ced*	*avārṣīt/varṣati/varṣiṣyati*	*vā*
Heaven noun nom.	if adverb	rain verb/ present/simp. fut. aorist/ 3^{rd}per.sing.no.	or part.

dhānyam	*avapsma/vapāmo/vapsyāmo*	*vā.*
Paddy noun accu.	sow verb aor./present/simp. future 1st pers. plu.no	or part.

If it were to rain, we would sow paddy.

Simple Future is used to indicate surprise in a sentence without having words **yacca** and **yatra**—

āścaryam	*andho*	*nāma*	*kṛṣṇam*	*drakhśyati.*
Wonder adverb	blind adj nomi. case	indecl.	Krishna noun accus. case sing.no.	see verb simp. fut. 3rd pers. sing.no.

Wonder a blind (person) sees Krishna.

Without using the word **yat** with root **smṛ**, a Simple Future is used in a sentence in the sense of Imperfect Past—

smarasi	*kṛṣṇa*	*gokule*	*vatsyāmaḥ.*
Remember	Krishna	Gokula	dwell
verb pres.	noun voc.	noun	verb simp. fut.
2nd pers	case	loc. case	1st pers. plu. no.
sing. no.		sing. no.	

Remember Krishna, we dwelt in Gokula.

Simple Future is used in option with Potential to express disbelief, shame etc.—

kaḥ	*harim*	*nindet/nindiṣyati.*
Who	Vishnu	speak ill
pers.pro.	noun accus.	verb pot.mood/simp. fut.
nom.	sing. no.	3rd per. sing. no.
sing. no.		

Who will speak ill of Vishnu?

With the use of word **kiṅkila** in the expression of great anger and disbelief Simple Future is used—

na	*śraddhe*	*na*	*marṣaye*	*vā*	*kiṅkila*
not	believe	not	endure	or	what a pity
neg.	verb pres.	neg.	verb pres.	part .	indecl.
part.	1st per. sing.	part.	1st pers.sing.		

tvam	*śūdrānna*	*bhokśyase.*
You pers.	the shudras noun	feed verb simp.
pro. 2nd pers	accu. case	future
sing. no.	plu. no.	2nd pers. sing. no.

I can neither believe nor endure that you will not feed the Shudras.

If doubt is expressed with particle **uta** or **api**, Simple Future is used—

uta	*daṇḍaḥ*	*patiṣyati.*
Particle	stick noun nomi.	fall verb simple
(doubt)	case	future 3rd pers.
		sing. no.

Will the stick fall. Or

api	*dhāsyati*	*dvāram.*
Particle (doubt)	shut verb simple future 3rd pers sing. no.	door noun accus. case sing. no.

Will he or she shut the door?

Similarly, with particle **alam** in the meaning of being sure, Simple Future is used—

alam	*kṛṣṇo*	*hastinam*	*haniṣyati.*
Surely particle	Krishna noun nomi. case	elephant noun accus. case sing. no.	kill verb simple future 3rd pers. sing. no.

Krishna will surely kill the elephant.

In a conditional sentence Simple Future is used optionally with the Potential Mood—

kṛṣṇam	*naṁsyati*	*cet*	*sukham*	*yāsyati.*
Krishna noun accus. sing.no.	submit verb simp.fut. 3rd pers. sing.no.	if cojun.	happiness noun accus.case sing.	get verb simp. fut.

Or

kṛṣṇam	*namet*	*cet*	*sukham*	*yāyāt.*
Krishna	submit verb poten.	if	happiness	get verb poten.

If one submits to Krishna, he will attain happiness.

Moods— There are four subjunctive moods in Sanskrit Language, namely; Imperative (**loṭ**), Potential (**liṅ**), Benedictive (**āśirliṅ**) and the Conditional (**lṛṅ**) **lakāra**.

Imperative Mood— The Imperative Mood indicates command, request, benediction, courteous enquiry, polite suggestion and much more. According to J.S. Speijer, "Sanskrit Imperative (loṭ) comprises more than is conveyed by its European name". (Sanskrit Syntax pg. 271) With second person all these abovementioned expressions are delivered in this mood—

1.	*jalam* Water noun accus. case sing. no.	*ānaya.* bring verb imper. mood 2nd pers. sing. no.

Bring water.

2.	*paritrāyasva* Help verb imper. mood 2nd pers. sing. no.	*paritrāyasva.* repetition of the same verb.

Help help!

3.	*hā* alas particle	*priyasakhi* dear friend noun voc. case sing.no.	*dehi* give verb imper. mood 2nd pers.sing.	*me* I pers. pro. dat. case sing.

priyavacanam.
sweet answer
adj. noun
accus. case
sing. no.

Alas my beloved, where are thou, please answer me!

4.	*putram* Son noun accus. case sing. no.	*labhasva* get verb imper. mood 2nd pers. sing. no.	*ātmaguṇānurūpam.* self reflexive pro. quality noun

Have a son with your qualities.

With the use of third person, the expression is generally blessing or gentle command—

1.	*parjanyaḥ* Cloud noun nomi. case	*kālavarṣī* time rain adj. of time noun	*bhavatu.* be verb imp. mood 3rd per. sing. no.

May rain pour down in time.

2. *śiśuḥ*	*svastho*	*bhavatu.*
Child noun nom. case mas. gen.	healthy adj.	be verb **imp. mood** 3rd per. **sing. no.**

The child should be healthy.

With the use of first person, generally there **is an** expression of question, binding or necessity;

1. *kim*	*karavāṇi*	*te.*
What int. pron.	do verb imp. mood 1st per. sing. no.	you dat. **case.** sing. no.

What should I do for you?

2. *vidyālayam*	*gacchāni*	*adya.*
School noun accu. case sing. no.	go verb imp. mood 1st per. sing. no.	today adv. of time

I must go to school today.

In the Imperative Mood, when frequency or repetition of act is indicated, the verb is repeated and it will be in the imperative 2nd person whereas the verb related to main subject may be in any tense—

1. *yāhi yāhi*	*iti*	*yāti.*
Go verb imp. mood. 2nd per. sing.no.repet.	thus adv.	go verb pres. tense 3rd pers. sing. no.

He goes often and often.

2. adhīṣva adhīṣva	iti	adhīte.
Study verb imper. mood 2nd pers. sing. no. repet.	thus adv.	study verb pres. tense 3rd pers. sing. no.

He studies again and again.

When several acts being done by a person are indicated, similar use of Imperative is done without repeating;

saktūn	*piba*	*dhānāḥ*	*khādetyabhyavaharati.*
barley accus. pl.	drink imper. 2nd pers.	corn accus. pl.	eat verb pres. 3rd pers. sing.

He takes his meal drinking barley and eating corn.

The Imperative is also used for commands and exhortations, the related time may be future or present. The expressions regarding this may be rules or laws or laying down percepts, as expressed by 'shall' or 'should' in English— bhavān yajatām (you should make an offering). Sometimes particles like **aṅga** and **hanta** are also used in this expression—

1.	*Hanta*	*prasīda*	*ānaya*	*tam.*
	well expr. parti.	please verb imper.	bring very imper 2nd pers. sing.	he pro. Accus. sing.

Well, bring him please.

2.	*Aṅga*	*avekśasva*	*saumitre.*
	Well parti.	look verb imper. 2nd pers. sing.	saumitra voc.

Come, look here Lakshaman.

In the use of courteous injunctions and requests, it is seen that 3rd person singular passive in Imperative is used instead of active 2nd person—

1.	*Bhadre*	*śīghram*	*ānīyatām*	*kśurabhāṇḍam.*
	Lady voc.	Quickly adv.	Fetch imper. 3rd pers. pass.	Razor box noun accus. sing.

O lady, quickly fetch me the razor box please.

2.	*ārye*	*itastāvat*	*āgamyatām.*
	dear voc.	here adv. till then parti.	come imper. 3rd pers. sing.pass.

O dear, please come here.

Another such polite expression of request is by using the verb **arhati** or **arhasi**—

kaścideṣāmupādhyāyasandeśastam devaḥ śrotum arhati. (they are here with their teacher´s message kindly listen, Sire!)

To indicate the expression of possibility or doubt, the use of Imperative is seen in the first and third person; rājan, kim te bhuyaḥ priyam karotu pākaśāsanaḥ (Vikram.v pg.184) O king, what more may Indra do for you? Or pratyetu kastad bhuvi! (utt. 1st canto) Who on earth will believe this?

For prohibition, the augment **mā** is seen in the use with the Imperative; mā paṭha (do not read), mā tvam vairāgyam gamaḥ (do not follow ascetism).

The Potential Mood

The Potential Mood in Sanskrit has varied expressions, command or directing a subordinate (vidhi), pressing invitation (nimantraṇa), giving permission to do something (āmantraṇa), telling a person respectfully to do some work (adhiṣta), politely asking a person a question (sampraśna) and prayer (prārthanā):

vidhi—

1. *tvam* / *pustakam* / *paṭheḥ.*
   you pro. nom. / book accus. / read verb poten, 2nd pers. sing.

   Read the book.

2. *Jalam* / *bhavān* / *ānayet.*
   Water noun accus. / you pro. nom. / bring verb poten. 3rd pers. honor.

   Please bring water.

nimantraṇa—

Iha / *bhavān* / *bhuñjīta.*
Here adv. / you pron. nom. / eat verb poten. 3rd pers. honor.

Your honour should take food here.

āmantraṇa—

ihāsīta / *bhavān*
Here adv. sit verb poten. / you pron. Nom.

3rd prs. sing.

You may sit here please.

adhīṣṭa—

putram	*adhyāpayet*	*bhavān.*
son noun accus. sing.	teach verb poten. 3rd pers. sing.	you pron. Nom.

You may please teach my son.

sampraśna—

kim	*bho*	*vedam*	*adhīyīya*	*uta*	*gaṇitam.*
What inte.	O expr.	the veda accus.	learn poten. 1st pers. sing.	or inde.	Math accus.

Sir, what shall I learn the Veda or Math?

prārthanā—

bho,	*bhojanam*	*labheya.*
O addr.	food accus.	get poten. 1st pers. sing. ques.

Can I get food, please?

All the abovementioned expressions are seen being used in Imperative also and that too, more often then in Potential Mood. The most common usage in Potential is of laying down precepts or rules or guidance as expressed by 'shall' or 'should' in English—

sahasā	*vidadhīta*	*na*	*kriyām.*
Quickly inde.	do verb poten. 3rd pers. sing.	not parti.	action noun accus. sing.

One should not act rashly. Or

āpadarthe	*dhanam*	*rakśhet.*
Bad time loc.	money accus. sing.	save verb poten. 3rd pers. sing.

One should save wealth against bad times. Or

ekaḥ	*svādu*	*na*	*bhuñjīta.*
One nume.	tasty adj. accus.	not inde.	eat verb poten. 3rd pers. sing.

One should not take sweetmeat alone.

There are other expressions also, such as may, might, could, will, would—

1.

Labheta	*sikatāsu*	*tailamapi*	*yatnataḥ*	*pīḍayan.*
Get verb poten. 3rd pers. sing.	sand noun loc. plu.	oil accus. inde.	effort adv.	squeeze verb particip.

One might even get oil from sand by diligently squeezing it.

2.

api	*girim*	*śirasā*	*bhindyāt.*
Even parti.	mountain noun accus.	head noun instr.	crack verb poten. 3rd pers. sing.

He might even crack the mountain with his head.

With the wonder expression, the Potential is used if **yadi** word is there in the sentence—

āścaryam	*yadi*	*so*	*adhīyīta.*
Wonder parti.	if indec.	he pron. nom.	study verb poten. 3rd pers. sing.

It is a wonder if he studies.

To express desire or wish, the Potential is used—

kāmo	*me*	*bhuñjīta*	*bhavān.*
desire noun	I pron. gen.	eat verb pote. 3rd pers.sing.	pron. honor.

It is my desire that you eat.

With the sense of expectation, **sambhāvanā**, the Potential is used optionally with the Simple Future—

sambhāvayāmi	*bhuñjīta*	*bhokśyate*	*vā*	*bhavān.*
expect verb	eat verb	Eat verb	Or	you
1st pers. sing.	pote.	simp. Fut.	part.	pron.
				honor.

I expect you will eat.

But only Potential will be used if yadi word is added in the sentence—

sambhāvayāmi	*yad*	*bhuñjīthāstvam.*
Expect verb	that adv.	eat verb poten.
1st pers. sing.		2nd pers. sing.
		you pron.

I expect that you will eat.

If **iṣ** or **prārth** verb is used to indicate wish, then Potential or Imperative Mood is used—

ichhāmi	*somam*	*pibet / pibatu*	*bhavān.*
Desire verb	Soma noun	drink verb	you pron.
1st pers.	accus. sing.	poten/	Nom. sing.
sing.		imper.	
		3rd pers.	

I wish your honour will drink Soma.

For showing the capability or fitness, the Potential Mood is used—

Tvam	*kanyām*	*vaheḥ.*
You pron. nom.	girl noun	marry verb
	accus. sing.	poten. Sing.

You are fit or capable to marry the girl. Or

Tvam	*bhāram*	*vaheḥ.*
You pron. nom.	load noun accus.	carry verb poten.
		2nd pers. sing.

You are capable to carry the load.

With the use of words api and uta in the meaning of mighty, the Potential Mood is used—

Uta /api	*vā*	*hanyād*	*agham*	*hariḥ.*
Definite	vā part.	.kill verb	sinful	Vishnu
part.		poten.	noun accus.	noun nom.
		3rd pers.		
		sing.		

Vishnu might definitely kill the demon.

The Potential is used in the sense of probability and possibility—

athavā	*mayi*	*gate*	*nṛśanso*	*hanyāt*	*enām.*
or indec.	I pron.	go verb	cruel	kill verb	she pron.
	loc.	parti.	noun	poten.	accus.
		sing.	nom.	Sing.	sing.

In my absence the cruel man may kill her. Or

Sakṛt	śrutam	ayam	bālaḥ	sarvam
Once adv.	here verb	This pron.	boy noun	all pron.
	partic.		nom.	sing.

cādhārayed	*hṛdi.*
And parti. retain	heart noun loc.
verb poten. 3rd pers. sing.	

This boy may retain all by heart what he has heard once.

The Potential also indicates doubt—

Kim	*uddiśya*	*bhagavatā*	*kāśyapena*	*matsakāśam*
What	purpose	Reverend	Kāshyap	I pron.
indec.	verb	noun instr.	noun instr.	gen. near
	partic.			Adv.

ṛṣayaḥ	*preṣitāḥ*	*syuḥ*
Rishi noun	send partic.	doubt verb poten.
nom. plu.		3rd pers. plu.

With what purpose may the Reverend Kashyap have sent the holy men to me?

In negative or interrogative sentences with improbability,

the Potential is used—

Nipuṇam	*anviṣyan*	*nopalabdhavān*	*katham*	*vā*	*upalabhyet.*
Well partic.	search verb partici.	not parti find verb partic.	how parti.	Or parti.	find verb poten. 3rd pers. sing.

He searched carefully but could not find him, how could he?

Potential is also used in a situation where agent of both actions is same—

bhuñjīya	*iti*	*ichhati.*
Eat verb poten. 1st pers. sing.	this indec.	desire verb pres. 3rd pers. sing.

He wishes that he will eat.

Referring time **'muhūrta'**, the Potential is used optionally with Imperative—

muhūrtād	*ūrdhvam*	*yajet / yajatām.*
time noun abl. sing.	after indec.	worship verb poten. / Imper.

Immediately afterwards, one should perform sacrifice.

The Benedictive Mood—

The Benedictive Mood is restricted to benedictions or blessings. For the expression of benediction, the Imperative Mood is also used—

Putraḥ	*te*	*bhavatāt / bhūyāt.*
Son noun nom.	you pron. geni. sing.	happen verb imper. / bened. 3rd pers. sing.

May you get a son. Or

Ciram	*jīvyatu / jīvyāt*	*bhavān.*
Long adv.	Live / bened. verb imper. / 3rd pers. sing.	you pron. honor.

May you live long.

The Benedictive is also used to express speaker's wish—

Kim	*anyad*	*āśāsmahe*	*kevalam*
What part.	else part.	wish verb bened. 1st pers. plu.	only indec.

vīraprasavā	*bhūyāḥ. (uttararamacaritam 1)*
Warrior noun birth noun (compound)	become verb bened. 2nd pers. sing.

What else shall we wish? May you give birth to a warrior.

The Conditional Mood—

The Conditional Mood expresses both future and past. When the non-performance of the action is involved and when the Potential can be used or where the falsity of the antecedent is involved, the Conditional Mood is used. It must be used both in antecedent as well as consequent sentences—

Suvṛṣtiśced	abhaviṣyad	tadā	subhikśam	abhaviṣyad.
Good rain noun if inde.	be verb condit.	Then part.	good crop noun	be 3rd pers. sing.

If there would be plenty of rain then there would be abundance of corn.

Conditional sentence can not be used where nearly a certain condition is implied, in such situation the sentence will take Potential Mood—

Yadi	*so'tra*	*sannihito*	*bhavet*	*tarhi*	*svadeśam*
If indec.	he pron. here adv.	present verb partic.	be cond.	then parti.	own part. country Accus. sing.

vīravad	*rakśet.*
Warrior like noun	protect verb poten.3rd pers. sing.

If he were here, he would protect his country bravely.

When a past action is indicated, the Conditional may be optionally used with Potential—

Katahm	*nāma*	*bhavān*	*dharmam*	*atyakśat / yajeḥ.*
How	indec.	you	religion	give up / poten.
part.		pron.	noun	cond. / 2nd pers.
		honor	accus.	past / sing.

How could you give up your religion?

The use of the Conditional Mood is found in Bhaṭṭ's literature to a great deal with the use of particles like **uta, api, jātu** etc.—

Api	*tatra*	*ripuḥ*	*sītām*	*nārthayiṣyat*	*durmatiḥ.*
If	there	enemy	Sita	not part.	evil noun
indec.	adv.	noun	noun	request	nom. sing.
		nom.	accus.	verb cond.	

if that evil enemy had not requested Sita. (Bhatt.xxi.8)

IV.2

Tense in Manipuri

Tense is a specified grammatical expression of location in time at which the action denoted by the verb occurs. Tense mainly involves concept of time as sequence depicting precedent and subsequent situations.

Aspect indicates the internal structure of an event or a situation, it is not concerned with relating time of the situation with other point of time. The difference between the two is like– one deals with the internal time, that is Aspect and the other deals with the external time, that is Tense. It is not necessary that every language has this grammatical device for showing location in time; Tense. Languages like Greek, Latin, Sanskrit have specific tense system but Tibeto-Burman languages like Manipuri do not seem to have tense system clearly, yet traditional Manipuri grammarians like Kalachanda Shastri, Nandlal Sharma, Dvijamani Dev Sharma are of the opinion that there is a distinct tense division in the form of Present, Past and Future and even their further units like Indefinite, Continuous, Perfect and Perfect Continuous in Manipuri language.

Tense in Manipuri is indicated by adverbial marker rather than by morphological marker. Below are given some examples—

1. *imā*   *ṅgarāṅ*   *ṅgā*   *thoṅṅi.*
   Mother   yesterday   fish   cook
   nom.   adv.mark.   accus.   past tense

   Mother cooked fish yesterday.

2. *imā*   *ṅgasi*   *ṅgā*   *thoṅṅi.*
   Mother   today   fish   cook
   nom.   adv. mark.   present tense.

Mother is cooking fish today.

3. *imā*	*hayeṅ*	*ṅgā*	*thoṅ gani.*
Mother	tomorrow	fish	cook
nom.	adv. mark.	accus.	future tense.

Mother will cook fish tomorrow.

From the above 1 and 2 sentences it is clear that time-difference (Present and Past) is indicated by adverbs like yesterday and today, whereas the verb is taking the same suffix. As in sentence 3 suffix used with the verb is different, adverbial time is used with this sentence also. Therefore the grammatical agreement between the verb and the adverbial time is evident in sentence 3, we do not see this arrangement in sentences 1 and 2.

Modern linguists are of the opinion that there are only two divisions of tense in Manipuri language— Future and Non-Future.

Future Tense—

In Manipuri language, an action which is going to take place in near future is classified in Future category. For this, marker '**gani**' is used after the verb ending with vowel and '**kani**' is used after the verb ending with consonant; for example—

1. *aikhoy*	*hayeṅ*	*ṅgā*	*cā gani.*
We	tomorrow	fish	eat
nom.	adv. mark.	accus.	future.

We shall eat fish tomorrow.

2. *ranjit*	*hāṅcit*	*coleg*	*cat kani.*
Ranjit	day after tomorrow	college	go
nom.	adv. mark.		future.

Rnjit will go to college day after tomorrow.

This type of application indicates **Indefinite Future**, the action may occur tomorrow or day after tomorrow. There is another type of Future-Continuous, for such situation suffixes '**ram**' or '**lam**' are used before '**gani**' or '**kani**'; for example—

1.	*shyāmā*	*na*	*leirik*	*pā ram gani.*
	Shyama	nom.	book accu.	read future con.

Shyama will be reading book.

2.	*binod*	*na*	*skul*	*cat lam gani.*
	Binod	nom.	school loc.	go future con.

Binod will be going to school.

This type of use (**lam**, **ram**) also shows the uncertainty of the action;

1.	*raman*	*na*	*ciṭṭhi*	*i ram gani.*
	Raman	nom.	letter accu.	write future.

Raman must have written the letter. (not sure)

2.	*mamā*	*na*	*cāk*	*thoṅ lam gani.*
	Mother	nom.	rice accu.	cook future.

Mother must have cooked food. (not sure)

'**Khi**' marker is also used to indicate the Future Continuous—

3.	*binoy*	*jagoi*	*sā khi gani.*
	Binoy nom.	dance accu.	perform future cont.

Binoy will continue to perform dance.

Future Perfect is also commonly used in Manipuri language. To show this situation, marker '**la**' is used in between '**ram/lam**' and '**gani/kani**'—

1.	*banita*	*na*	*thabak*	*loi ram la gani.*
	Banita	nom.	work accu.	finish future perfect.

Banita will have finished the work.

2.	*aṅgāṅ*	*na*	*saṅgom*	*thak lam la gani.*
	Child	nom.	milk accu.	drink future perfect.

Child will have drunk milk.

Immediate Future—

Marker '**ge**' and '**ke**' is used to indicate the immediate future.

1. *ai* *haujik* *lākke.*
   I nom. now adv.mark. come imm. future.

   I will come now.

2. *radha* *gita* *pāge.*
   Radha nom. Gita accu. read imm. future.

   Radha will read the Gita.

Marker '**dori**' fixed after verb + **ga** is also in use to indicate the near future;

radha *gita* *pā ga dori.*
Radha nom. Gita accu. read near future.

Radha is about to read the Gita.

Modern linguists are of the opinion that markers like **ram**, **lam**, **la**, **ga**, **khi** etc. come in the category of Aspectual Markers.

Non-Future—

The Non –Future category comprises the events taking place in different situations, hence the linguists classify this in the Aspect category, not the Tense. In their opinion, a situation can be divided in four units—1. Simple or Habitual expression 2. Progressive action (the event is going on), 3. Perfect—the action has already taken place, and in the fourth unit that is the Unrealised Aspect— action is going to happen in future. This Future has already been discussed in Tense, yet it will be appropriate only to include its divisions like Indefinite, Progressive etc in Aspect category.

Simple Aspect—

Simple Aspect is used to express simple statement, habitual thing or universal truth. The markers used in this

Aspect are,—**ni**,— **y**,—**mi** —**pi**, —**li** etc. These markers are fixed to the verbs with some phonological order. Suffix **y** is attached to the verb ending with K consonant, rest of the suffixes follow the same nasal consonant in the verb, for example—

1. *aṅgāṅ* *saṅgom* *thak—y.*
   Child nom. milk accu. drink aspect simple.

   Child drinks milk.

2. *mamā* *na* *cāk* *thoṅ —ṅi.*
   Mother nom. rice accu. cook aspect simple.

   Mother cooks rice.

3. *lata* *kanna* *kap—pi.*
   Lata nom. a lot adj. cry aspect simple.

   Lata cries a lot.

4. *baby* *khoṅ* *cat—li.*
   Baby nom. foot inst. walk aspect simple.

   Baby walks on foot.

In this last sentence suffix **li** follows verb ending with **t**, hence this suffix can take both **t/l** in the end of the verb.

Progressive Aspect—

Progressive Aspect expresses the continuation of action. It takes suffixes **ri** and **li** with the verb. Suffix **ri** occurs after verb ending with vowel and **li** after verb ending with consonant, for example—

1. *lata* *haujik* *cāk* *cā—ri.*
   Lata nom. now adv. mark. rice accu. eat aspect cont.

   Lata is eating rice now.

2. *sona* *isai* *sak—li.*
   Sona nom. song accu. sing aspect cont.

   Sona is singing song now.

3. *ranjit* *ciṭṭhi* *i—ri.*

Ranjit nom. letter accu. write aspect cont.

Ranjit is writing letter.

Perfect Aspect—

Perfect Aspect indicates that the action is already done or completed. It takes two markers **re** or **le**. Suffix **re** follows vowel-ending verb, whereas **le** follows consonant-ending verb. Besides these two suffixes, —**me**,—**ne**, —**pe**, etc also occur after the verb ending with the same consonant, for example; —**me** occurs after **m** ending verb and so on and so forth—

1. *bijoy* *na* *hai* *cā—re.*
   Bijoy nom. fruit accus. eat aspect perfect.

   Bijoy ate fruit.

2. *aṅgāṅ* *na* *leirik* *pā—re.*
   Child nom. book accus. read aspect perfect.

   Child read the book.

3. *aikhoy* *na* *pāo* *tam—me.*
   We nom. news accus. learn aspect perfect.

   We learnt the news.

4. *mahāk* *na* *yensāṅ* *taṅ—ṅe.*
   She nom. curry accus. taste aspect perfect.

   She tasted the curry.

5. *aṅgāṅ* *na* *hui* *cup—pe.*
   Child nom. dog accus. kiss aspect perfect.

   Child kissed the dog.

Suffix– **khre** is used to indicate the completion of action. Use of— **khre** indicates that the speaker is sure about the certainty of the action;

1. *makhoy* *dilli* *cat—khre*
   They nom. delhi loc. go aspect perfect.

   They have gone to Delhi.

2. *haudoṅ* *na* *saṅgom* *thak-khre.*
   Cat nom. milk. accus. drink aspect perfect.

   Cat has drunk milk.

There is another usage in the Perfect Aspect; the continuity of the Perfect action—has been doing etc. This Aspect is known as Perfect Progressive Aspect. This is denoted by **rammi/ramli** and **lammi/lamli**;

1. *radha* *cāk* *thoṅ—lamli.*
   Radha nom. rice. accus. cook aspect perfect progressive.

   Radha has been cooking rice.

2. *bindiya* *leirik* *pā—rammi.*
   Bindiya nom. book accus. read aspect perfect progressive.

   Bindiya has been reading book

Mood—

Mood is related to the application of the verb or manner in which the verb has been used. Manipuri has Mood also as we find in other languages. There are three major Moods recognized by linguists in Manipuri language, namely—

1. Imperative Mood
2. Potential Mood
3. Subjunctive Mood

Imperative Mood—

Imperative Mood expresses command, request to the second and third person. Permission or willingness to let the work be done is also intended when it is used in First Person. For command to the Second Person, suffix –**ro**/—**lo** is used in the expression of persuation or endearment, whereas suffix –**ru**/—**lu** is supposed to be used as general command to the junior. Suffixes —**ro** or –**ru** occurs after verb ending with vowel and –**lo** or –**lu** after verb ending with consonant. Sometimes only —**o** or –**u** is used in this

Mood. These suffixes have other allomorphs also; —**mo**, —**no**, —**po** or –**mu**, —**nu**, —**pu** etc. when the verb is ending with the same consonant—**m**, **n**, **p** respectively.

1. *naṅ* *cāk* *cā-ro.*
   You food det. eat command.

   You eat food.

2. *haujik* *skul* *cat-lo.*
   Now adv. mark. school locative. go command.

   Go to school now.

3. *naṅ* *yum* *cat-lo.*
   You home loc. go command.

   Go home.

4. *naṅ* *leirik* *pā-ru.*
   You book det. read command.

   Read book.

5. *naṅ* *ceṅ* *cām-mo.*
   You rice det. wash command.

   Wash rice.

6. *naṅ* *phamuṅ* *da* *ḥip-po.*
   You bed loc. lie command.

   Lie on the bed.

7. *masi* *aṅgāṅ* *bu* *phu-u.*
   This adj. child accus. beat command.

   Beat this child.

With the Third Person suffix **sanu** is added to the verb;

1. *aṅgāṅ* *cāk* *cā-sanu.*
   Child rice det. eat command.

   Let the child eat rice.

2. *makhoy* *yum* *da* *lāk-sanu.*
   They home loc. come command.

   Let them come home.

When this **sanu** suffix is added to the stative verb like **iṅ**—cold, **mot**—dirty etc, it gives the meaning of indifference or warning;

1. *mahāk* *iṅ-sanu.*
   He/she cold command.

   Let him/her suffer from cold.

2. *banita* *ṅgāo-sanu.*
   Banita naughty command.

   Let Banita be naughty.

With the First Person **si** suffix is used, when the speaker proposes to initiate the action;

1. *aikhoy* *haujik* *yum* *cat-si.*
   We now adv. mark. home loc. go initiation.

   Let us go home now.

2. *aikhoy* *si* *sup* *loina* *thak-si.*
   We this soup det. together drink initiation.

   Let us drink up this soup.

Potential Mood—

Potential Mood is indicated by the expression—to permit, to be able, have got to do or being responsible for; the suffixes for these expressions are used as ' **yāba**, **ṅgamba**, **thokpa** and **tāba'** respectively. The examples are—

1. *damo* *catpa* *yāre.*
   Damo go permit mood potential.

   Damo is permitted to go.

2. *monika* *office* *da* ' *phamba yāre.*
   Monika office loc. sit permit mood potential.

   Monika is permitted to (may) sit in the office.

When suffix **yā** is prefixed with **ram/lam**, added to the verb, it indicates the speculation.

1. *tamo sabita da ciṭṭhi pi ramba yare.*
Brother Sabita dative letter give speculation mood potential.

Brother might give letter to Sabita.

2. *ayi si pot puba ṅgammi.*
I this thing deter. carry able mood potential.

I can carry this thing.

3. *naṅ na bu parikhā thok i.*
You exam deter. give mood potential.

You should give exam.

4. *naṅ na asi thabak loisanba tāre.*
You this work det. finish (fall upon) potential mood.

You must finish this work.

Use of suffix '**oiba**' is also seen for the same use— got to do or morally obliged;

naṅ na asi thabak loisanba oi/tāy. (suffix '**tāy**' also gives the same meaning).

Subjunctive Mood—

This Mood indicates condition—if, in case etc, the suffixes used for this purpose are '**rabadi/labadi** or **rabasu/labasu** for the meaning of though or although. The examples are—

1. *mahāk na phu rabadi naṅ na kap-kani.*
He/she beat condition you cry future tense.

If he/she beats, you will cry.

2. *mamā na sima da hāi-rabasu, mahāk na*
Mother Sima dat. say cond. she nom.

leirik pā de.
book read
past tense neg.

Although mother asked Sima, she did not study.

There is another expression in the Subjunctive Mood; that is Contingent Tense. In this expression suffix **'ram'** is added to the suffix **'labadi** or **rabadi'**. **'Ram** or **lam'** is used in both the clauses but Future Tense is taken by the second clause only. **'Ram'** again has allomorphs like **'lam**. **nam** etc;

1.	*misa na*	*cāk*	*thoṅ*	*ṅgam badi,*
	Misa nom.	food	cook	subjunctive potential

Sana na	*cā ram gani.*
Sana nom.	eat future perfect.

If Misa had cooked food, Sana would have eaten.

2.	*Bino na*	*leirik*	*kanna*	*pā ram labadi*
	Bino	book	hard	study subj. potential

mahāk na	*parikhā*	*pās tau-ram-gani.*
he nom.	exam	clear future perfect.

If Bino had studied hard, he would have cleared the exam.

Besides these above said moods, Optative Mood has also been discussed by linguists. This Mood shows the speaker's desire or intention to initiate some action;

1.	*ayi*	*hayeṅ*	*skul*	*cat-ke.*
	I nom.	tomorrow adv. mark.	school	go optative.

I intend to go to school tomorrow.

Suffix **'toi** or **doi'** is also used for the same purpose;

2.	*ayi*	*leirik*	*pā-doi-ni.*
	I nom.	book	read optative.

I intend to read book.

This condition of Optative Mood has also been inducted in Future Tense by some grammarians. Some linguists have talked about Assumptive Mood also in which suffixes **'gani/kani'** follow suffix **'ram**,' attached to the verb;

1. *sarita* *skul da* *lei-ram-gani.*
   Sarita nom. school loc. be assumptive mood.

   Sarita must be in the school.

Grammarians like A. J. Primrose, Nandlal Sharma include both these moods in Future Tense only. They do not consider these two in the category of Mood.

Conclusion

Sanskrit and Manipuri, both languages have Tense in grammatical system, though it is not as specific in Manipuri as in Sanskrit. Adverbial markers make the sentence more complete than the suffix used with the verb denoting various locations in time. Sanskrit has very fine division of each Tense and abundant use of this pattern is seen in Sanskrit literature.

In Manipuri language, Aspect signifies the situations taking place more specifically like Simple, Progressive etc. We do not find Progressive Aspect as such in Sanskrit. In fact, Tense only takes care of Progressive situations and the adverb of time is used to indicate this. Sanskrit does not have Perfect Progressive Aspect also.

Both Sanskrit and Manipuri languages have Mood. Imperative and Potential Moods are used in the same manner in both the languages, Imperative deals with the expressions of willingness, permission, command generally and Potential deals with the expressions of being responsible for, got to do etc. What is discussed in Subjunctive Mood in Manipuri, is discussed in Conditional Mood in Sanskrit. This Subjunctive has vast application in Manipuri. The conditions which have been accepted in Optative Mood by some linguists in Manipuri language, are also prevalent in Potential Mood in Sanskrit. The Assumptive Mood accepted by some linguists or Future Tense by others, is a unique aspect in Manipuri language.

V.1

Case in Sanskrit

Sanskrit grammarians have recognized eight cases in Sanskrit. They are described here with their terminations or **vibhaktis**; Nominative (prathamā) Accusative (dvitīyā), Instrumental (tritiyā), Dative (caturthī), Ablative (pañcami), Genitive (ṣaṣṭhī), Locative (saptamī) and Vocative Case (sambodhana). The arrangement of these cases is according to the magnitude of the similarity to one another. There are eight cases but **kārakas** corresponding to these cases are six, since kāraka is defined as the joining factor of a noun/pronoun and a verb. According to Apte," Kāraka is the name given to the relation subsisting between a noun and a verb in a sentence." Hence Genitive Case which is not directly related to the verb, is not considered a kāraka by grammarians. The **vibhaktis** are used in Sanskrit grammar in other areas also, besides corresponding the specified **kāraka.**

1. Nominative Case (prathamā vibhakti)— Nominative case is termed as **kartā kāraka**. This case is mainly the naming case. In this case, Kartā is the agent or doer of the action. When the agent or subject is used in Nominative case, the predicate is also used in the same case, for example.

(i)	*kumbhakārakaḥ*	*ghaṭam*	*karoti.*
	The potter	pitcher	create
	noun nom.	noun accus.	verb tran. pres. 3rd pers.sing.no.

The potter creates (a) pitcher.

(ii)	*s'yāmā*	*pustakam*	*paṭhati.*

Shyama	book	read
noun nom.	noun accus.	verb tran. pres. 3rd per. sing. no

Shyama reads (the) book.

In both the above sentences the verbs **karoti** and **paṭhati** represent the doer or kartā.

The Nominative also signifies a noun independently; ghaṭah (pitcher), patram (leaf), nadī (river) etc.

In passive mode also, the object takes Prathamā vibhakti—

S'akuntalayā	*mṛgaśāvakaḥ*	*sevyate.*
Shakuntala	fawn	attend
noun ins.kartā	noun nom.obj	V.tran.pres.pass. 3rd per.sing.no.

The fawn is attended by Shakuntala.

2. Accusative case (dvitiyā vibhakti)— Accusative case is known as **karma kāraka.** It indicates the object of the transitive verb—

kapiḥ	*kadalīphalam*	*khādati.*
Monkey	banana	eat
noun nom.	noun accus.obj	V. tran. pres. act.3rd Per.sing.no

Monkey is eating banana.

Sometimes intransitive verb also requires object—

Aham	*gṛham*	*gacchāmi.*
I	home	go
pronoun nom	noun accus.obj	V. intr. act. pres, 1st per.sing.no

I am going home.

All verbs indicating **motion,** require dvitiyā vibhakti.

An intransitive root acts as a transitive root if it is preceded by a preposition, and then it takes dvitiyā vibhakti—

1. *vaikuṅṭhạm adhyāste hariḥ.*

vaikuṅṭhạm	*adhyāste*	*hariḥ.*
Heaven	dwell	Vishnu.
noun accus.	v+prep.intr.pres.simp. 3rd pers. sing. no.	nom. case

Vishnu dwells in heaven.

2. *sanmārgam abhiniviśate.*

sanmārgam	*abhiniviśate.*
Right way	follow
obj.dvi	v.intr.pres.simp 3rd pers. sing. no

He/she follows the right way.

A verb may take more than one object also in a sentence; in that case both the objects take dvitiyā vibhakti—

(i)

guruḥ	*chātram*	*pras'nam*	*pracchati.*
Teacher	student	question	ask
nom	dvi.obj	dvi.obj	V.tr.pres,simp. 3rd pers.sing.no

The teacher asks the student a question.

(ii)

nyāyādhīśaḥ	*abhiyuktam*	*pañcalakśarūpykam*
Judge	convict	five lakh rupees
nom	dvi.obj	dvi.obj

daṅḍayati.
fine
V.tr pres.simp. 3rd pers.sing.no

Judge fines the convict for rupees five lakh.

Sometimes, in a sentence there is an unwanted action which is not consciously done, the object of such action also requires accusative marker, for example—

Gṛham	*gacchan*	*tṛṇam*	*spṛśati.*
Home	go	grass	touch
dvi.obj	part.pres	dvi.obj.unwan	v.tr.pres simp. 3rd pers sing.

He/she touches grass while going home.

Here the most desired object of the action is **gṛha**, the

undesired object is **tṛṇa**, but both the objects demand accusative marker.

The accusative can also be seen in adverbial constructions—

Sā	*pañcakilomīṭaram*	*calati.*
She	five kilometer	walk
Pron. nom	adv.dvi.	v.intr.pres.simp. 3rd pers.sing.no

She walks five kilometer.

When words like **ubhayataḥ** (both sides), **sarvataḥ** (everywhere), **abhitaḥ** (this side) or double forms like **uparyupari** (above), **adho'dhaḥ** (below) are used in a sentence, it is ruled by **dvitiyā vibhakti**.

The examples are—

(i)	*vidyālayam*	*sarvataḥ*	*gṛhāḥ*	*santi.*
	School	all sides	houses	are
	Noun obj.dvi	prep.	nom.mas.gen	ver.intr. 3rd pers.plur.no

Houses are there on all sides of the school.

(ii)	*pṛthvīm*	*adho'dhaḥ*	*jalam*	*asti.*
	Earth	below	water	is
	obj.dvi	prep.	nom.neu.gen.	ver. intr. pres. 3rd per sing.no.

There is water below the earth.

If **dhik** word is used in a sentence, it takes **dvitiyā vibhakti,** for example—

Dhik	*tvām*	*mūrkham.*
Fie	you	fool
interj.	obj.dvi.	accus.2nd pers sing.

Fie upon thee fool.

Use of words **antarā** (between) and **antareṇa** (without) requires dvitiyā **vibhakti** in a sentence—

(i)

Mām ca	*tvām ca*	*antarā*	*kṛṣṇaḥ.*
I	you and	between	Krishna
obj.dvi. 1st pers. sing.no. conj	2nd pers. sing.no. conj	prep.	nom. 3rd pers sing. no.

There is Krishna between you and me.

(ii)

na	*tvām*	*antareṇa*	*ko'pi*	*kartum*	*śaktaḥ*
Not	you	without	whoever	to do	able
neg. part.	dvi. 2nd pers.	prep.	nom. 3rd pers sing.	ver.part.	adj.

Nobody has the ability to do this except you.

Prepositions like **anu** (after), **abhi** (before), **upa** (near, inferior) take **dvitiyā vibhakti** in a sentence, for example—

(i)

japam	*anu*	*prāvarṣat.*
Prayer	after	rain
dvi 3rd pers.	prep.	ver.past3rd pers. sing. no.

It rained after the prayers.

(ii)

anu	*harim*	*surāḥ.*
After	Vishnu	gods
prep.	dvi 3rd pers	nom.3rd pers. plu. verb hidden.

Gods come after Vishnu.

(iii)

upa	*harim*	*surāḥ.*
After	Vishnu	gods
prep.	dvi.3rd pers. sing no.	nom.3rd pers plu.

Gods are inferior to Vishnu.

The marker in this case is **am** in singular number and **ān** in plural number, it varies in several nouns and in different genders; sometimes it is not visible—**vāri, nadī.**

3. Instrumental Case (Tritīyā Vibhakti)—

Instrumental case is applied either with the agent (passive mode) or with the tool; medium of the action, it takes tritīyā vibhakti—

(i)

Rāmeṇa	*bāṇena*	*hataḥ*	*bāliḥ.*
Rama	arrow	kill	Bali
agen.pass.tri	tool, instr. sing.	ver.pass.3rd per.	obj.pratha. sing.

Bali was killed with an arrow by Rama.

(ii)

rañjanā	phenilena	mukham	prakśhālayati.
Ranjana	soap	face	clean
nom.sing.	instr.sing.	obj.dvi. sing.	ver. pres.3rd per.sing.

Ranjana cleans face with soap.

The marker in this case is **ena** and **eiḥ** (masculine, neuter gender), **ayā** and **bhiḥ** (feminine) in singular and plural numbers. **Bhyām** is the common dual number.

The instrumental case is also used as 'sociative'; together with or accompanied by—

Janāḥ	*mitreiḥ*	*samam*	*anurañjanti.*
People	friends	with	enjoy
nom.plur	ass.instr.plu.	ass.mark	ver.pres.3rd per plu.no.

People feel happy in the company of their friends.

The sociative is generally followed by words like, **saha, sākam, sārdham**, **samam.**

Tritiyā vibhakti is also used for comparing, finding similarity; in such a situation words like **tulyaḥ, sadṛśaḥ, samānaḥ** are added with the noun to be compared—

Prajñayā	*sadṛś*	*āgamaḥ.*
Intellect	according	learning
tri.comp.3rd pers.	adj.	nom. 3rd pers. sing.

Their learning was according to the intellect. (raghuvaṁśa 1st canto).

Words like '**rahitaḥ, hīnaḥ, vihitaḥ, viyuktaḥ**' also command **tritīyā vibhakti**—

rāmeṇa	*viyuktaḥ*	*daśarathaḥ*	*svargam*	*agamat.*
Rama	separate	Dasharath	heaven	go
tri.3rd pers.	adj.	nom.3rd pers.	obj.3rd pers.	ver. past sing.

Dasharath died after being separated from Ram.

In Sanskrit, the Instrumental case is widely and largely used in varied situations; for purpose—

Sā	*adhyayanena*	*chhātrāvāse*	*vasati.*
She	study	hostel	live
nom.femi.	pur.instr.	sapt.neu. gend.	verb pres 3rdper. sing.

Because of study she lives in the hostel.

Abstract noun for being the reason—

sandīpaḥ	*jvareṇa*	*grastaḥ.*
Sandeepa	fever	grip
nom. mas.gen.	reas.tri.sing.	ver.pres.parti. 3rd pers.sing.

Sandeepa is down with fever.

Words depicting nature/characteristic take **tritīyā vibhakti**—

(i)

Madhuḥ	*prakṛtyā*	*madhuraḥ*	*asti.*
Honey	nature	sweet	is
nom mas. gen	tri.femi.gen	nom.mas.gen.	ver.3rdper. sing. no.

Honey is sweet by nature.

(ii)

ātankavādi	*svabhāvena*	*krūraḥ*	*vartate.*
Terrorist	nature	cruel	is
nom.sing.	tri.mas. gen	nom.	ver. pre 3rd per.sing.

Terrorist is cruel by nature.

The body part, having a handicap requires **tritīyā vibhakti**—

Śakuniḥ	*pādena*	*khañjaḥ*	*āsīt.*
Shakuni	foot	lame	was
nom.sing.	tri.sing.	adj.nom.	ver.past.3rd per.sing.

Shakuni had difficulty in walking.

Words like **'alam, kṛtam'** in the meaning of enough take **tritīyā vibhakti**—

Alam	*vivādena.*
Enough inde.	debate tri.mas.gen.3rd per. sing.

Enough of debate.

Tritīyā vibhakti is used when words like **kim, kāryam, arthaḥ, prayojanam** in the meaning of use or need are in a sentence—

Tṛṇena	*kāryam*	*bhavati*	*īśvarāṇām.*
Grass	purpose	is	rich people
tri.sing.	nom.neu.	ver.pres. 3rd per. sing.	ṣaṣṭ.mas. plu.

A blade of grass also serves the purpose of the rich people.

When accomplishment of work is expressed in the sentence, words indicating time and place take tritīyā vibhakti—

Saḥ	*pañcavarṣeiḥ*	*āyurvijñānam*	*adhītavān.*
He	five years time,	medical science	learn
nom. sing.	tri.plu.	obj. sing.	3rd per. sing.

He studied medical science for five years.

4. Dative Case (Caturthī Vibhakti)—

Dative is the indirect object for which or whom something is done or given, it is known as **sampradāna kāraka** –

(i) mātā bhikśukāya bhojanam yacchati.

Mother	beggar	food	give
nom.sing.	obj.catur. sing.	obj. dir. sing.	ver.pres. 3rd per sing.

Mother gives food to the beggar.

(ii)

devadattāya	*gām*	*pratiśṛṇoti.*
Devadatta	cow	promise
ind.obj.dat. sing.	dir.obj sing.	ver.pres. 3rd pers. sing.

He/she promises to give a cow to Devadatta.

The Dative Case is used to indicate an action or a state, for example—

Ārtratrāṇāya	*vaḥ*	*śastram.*
protection of the distressed action, dat.sing.	you 2nd pers. pro. sing.	weapon noun neu. gen. sing.

Your weapon is for the protection of the distressed.

There are several states in which the Dative Case is used;

—to like, please,

Bālakāya	*miṣṭānnam*	*rocate.*
Child	sweetmeat	like
dat.sing.	prath.sing.	ver. pres.3rd per. sing.

Child likes the sweetmeat.

—to long for,

Kāntā	ābhūṣaṇebhyaḥ	spṛhyati.
Kanta	jwellary	long
nom.sing.	obj.catu. plu.	ver. pres.3rd per. sing.

Kanta longs for jwellary.

—to owe to a person,

rañjanāya *pañcaśatam* *dhārayati.*

Ranjana	five hundred	owe
catu.sing.	dvi.sing.	ver.pres.3rd.pers. sing.

He/she owes Rs. five hundred to Ranjan.

—to be angry with, having malice etc (krudh, druha, īrṣya)

(i)	*mātā*	*bālakāya*	*krudhyati.*
	Mother	child	angry
	nom.sing.	dat.sing.	ver. pres.3rd pers. sing.

Mother is angry with the child.

(ii)	*duryodhanaḥ*	*pāṇḍavebhyaḥ*	*druhyati.*
	Duryodhana	Pandava	deceive
	nom.sing.	noun,dat.plu.	ver.pres.3rd per. sing.

Duryodhana deceives Pandavas.

'alam' word to indicate enough, sufficient—

Devebhyo	*hariḥ*	*alam.*
Gods	Vishnu	enough
noun catu. plu.	noun nom.	indeclinable

Vishnu is enough for gods.

—for hailing, salutation,

(i)	*gurave*	*namaḥ.*
	Teacher noun catur.	salutation noun sing.

Salutation (is offered) to the teacher.

(ii)	*svasti*	*prajābhyaḥ.*
	Hail noun fem.	people noun catur. plu.

Hail to the people.

The Dative Case is also used to indicate purpose or aim—

rādhā	*phalebhyo*	*yāti*	*āpaṇaṁ.*
Radha	fruits	go	shop
nom. sing.no.	noun dat.plu.	ver.pres. 3rd per.sing.no.	obj. dvi.sing.no.

Radha goes to the shop for fruits.

Or

ghāṭebhyaḥ	*mṛttikā*	*vartate.*
Pitcher	soil	be
noun dat.plu.	noun nom. sing.	ver.pres.3rd pers. sing.

Soil is (there) for pitchers.

With words like 'bhadram, kuśalam' in the expression of blessing, greeting

Caturthī vibhakti is used—

svāgatam	*bhavadbhyo.*
Welcome	you
noun neu. prath. sing.	pers. pron. catu. plu. respect.

Welcome you.

Verbs like '**kath, vid with ni upasarga** require caturthī vibhakti—

ārye,	*kathayāmi*	*te*	*bhūtārtham.*
O worthy lady	tell	you	truth
interj. voc. noun	ver. pres. 1st per sing.	pro. catur.	noun nom. sing.

O worthy lady, I tell you the truth.

With root '**man**'in the meaning of **think** (contempt), caturthī vibhakti is used optionally in the indirect object—

na	*tvām*	*tṛṇam/tṛṇāya*	*manye.*
Not	you	straw	consider
neg. Parti.	obj. pers. pro.	noun dvi/catur. sing.	ver. pres.

I do not consider you to be worthy of a straw.

Roots in the meaning of motion require **caturthī vibhakti** optionally, only when physical movement is involved—

Chātrāḥ	*vidyālayam/vidyalayāya*	*gacchanti.*
Student	school	go
nom.plu.	obj.dvi/catur.sing.	ver.pres. 3rd per. plu.

Students go to school.

5. Ablative Case (Pañcamī Vibhakti)—

In Sanskrit Ablative Case is **apādāna kāraka**, it takes **pañcamī vibhakti.** It is used to indicate separation from a person, thing or place—

(i)	*Rañjanaḥ*	*dhāvato*	*basayānāt*	*patitaḥ.*
	Ranjan	run	bus	fall
	nom.sing.	ver.parti.	pañc.sing.	ver.pas.part. 3rd pers.sing.

Ranjan fell from the running bus.

(ii)	*adhunā*	*pravīnā*	*gṛhāt*	*āyāti.*
	Now	Praveena	house	come
	indec.	nom.sing.	pañc. sing.	ver.pres.3rd per.sing.

Now Praveena is coming from the house.

(iii)	*pāpāt*	*nivārayati.*
	Bad deed	stop
	pañc.sing.	ver.pres.3rd. pers. sing.

(good company) keeps one off from bad deeds.

Ablative Case is used for indicating the origin, birth—

(i)	*Himālayāt*	*gaṅgā*	*prabhavati.*
	Himalaya	Ganga	originate
	ablat.sing.	nom.sing.	ver.pres.3rd pers.sing.

The Ganga originates from the Himalayas.

(ii)	*gomayāt*	*vṛścikaḥ*	*jāyate.*
	Cowdung	scorpion	born
	ablat.sing.	nom.sing.	ver.pres.3rd pers.sing.

Scorpion is born out of cowdung.

Ablative Case is used in different situations—

For indicating comparision,

(i)	*Jananī*	*janmabhūmiśca*	*svargādapi*	*garīyasī.*
	Mother	and motherland	heaven also	great
	nom.sing.	nom.sing.	ablat.sing.	com. adj.

Mother and motherland are greater than heaven.

(ii)	*aśvamedhasahasrebhyaḥ*	*satyameva*	*atiricyate.*
	Thousand horse sacrifice	truth	superior
	pañc.com.plu.	nom. sing.inde.	ver.pres.3rd per.sing.

Truth is superior to thousand horse sacrifices.

For indicating envy (spṛhā), refrain (virāma), abhorance (jugupsā), swerving (pramāda) etc.—

(i)	*duryodhanaḥ*	*pāṇḍavebhyaḥ*	*spṛhyati.*
	Duryodhan	Pandavas	envy
	nom.sing.	pañc.plu.	ver.pre. 3rd pers. sing.

Duryodhan envies Pandavas.

(ii)	*raghuvīraḥ*	*adharmāt*	*viramati.*
	Raghuveer	bad deed	refrain
	nom.sing.	pañc.sing.	ver.pres.3rd. per. sing.

Raghuveer refrains from bad deeds.

For indicating fear, protection from danger—

(i)	*Śiśuḥ*	*sarpād*	*bibheti.*
	Child	snake	fear
	nom. sing.	pañc.sing.	ver.pres.3rd pers. sing.

The child is afraid of snake.

(ii) *rakśakaḥ* *rajanīm* *duścaritrāt* *rakśati.*

Policeman	Rajani	bad character	protect
nom.sing.	obj.dvi.sing.	pañc.sing.	ver.pres.3rd pers. sing.

The policeman protects Rajani from bad character.

For hiding, warding—

(i)	*mātuḥ*	*nilīyate*	*kṛṣṇaḥ.*
	Mother	hide	Krishna
	pañc.sing.	ver.pres.3rd. pers.sing.	nom. sing.

Krishna is hiding from mother.

(ii)	*yavebhyaḥ*	*gām*	*vārayati*	*kṛṣakaḥ.*
	Barley	cow	ward off	farmer
	pañc. plu.	obj.dvi. sing.	ver.pres.3rd pers. sing.	nom.sing.

The farmer wards off the cow from barley.

For indicating distance (far/near) Ablative Case is used optionally—

hāṭaḥ	*mama*	*gṛhāt/gṛhasya*	*dūram*	*asti.*
Market	I	house	far	be
nom.sing.	ṣaṣthi sing.	pañc/ṣaṣṭḥi sing.	indecl.	ver. pres. 3rd pers. sing.

Market is far from my house.

For indicating abstract noun as reason or cause of action, Ablative is used optionally—

pāṭaccaraḥ	*jāḍyena/jāḍyāt*	*baddhaḥ.*
Pickpocket	foolishness	catch
nom.sing.	trit. pañc.sing.	ver.past part. 3rd pers. sing.

The pickpocket was caught because of his foolishness.

For words like prabhṛti/ārabhya (starting with), bahiḥ (outside), param (after)

Ablative case is used–

(i)

Śaiśavāt	*prabhṛti*	*poṣitām.*
Childhood	since	brought up
ablat.sing.	indec.	ver.past part. fem. gend. dvi.sing.

(She was) brought up since her childhood.

(ii)

āmūlāt	*śrotum*	*icchāmi.*
Beginning	hear	desire
ablat.sing.	ver.parti.	ver.pres.1st pers. sing.

I want to hear since beginning.

6. Genitive Case (Ṣaṣṭhī Vibhakti)—

In Sanskrit Genitive Case is mainly used for indicating possession, belonging, partaking. It is connected with the noun/pronoun which dominates the action of the sentence; hence it is not treated as a **kāraka**, for example—

(i)

rājñaḥ	*putraḥ.*
King gen. sing.	son nom.sing.

Son of a king. Or

(ii)

ghaṭasya	*kārakaḥ.*
Pitcher gen. sing.	maker nom.sing.

Maker of the pitcher.

(iii)

mama	*pustakam.*
I gen. sing.	book prath.sing.

My book.

(iv)

skhalanam	*manuṣyāṇām*	*dharmaḥ.*
Err	men	nature
nom.sing.	gen.plu.	prath.sing.

To err is human.

Ṣaṣṭhī Vibhakti is used at different places, such as—

With verbs like **iś, bhū** with **pra** upasarga in the

meaning of rule, govern—

(i)	*yadi*	*prabhaviṣyāmi*	*ātmanaḥ.*
	If	control	self
	indec.	ver.future 1st per.sing.	ṣaṣṭhī, poss. pron.sing.

If I am able to control myself.

With words like **tulyaḥ, sadṛśaḥ** in the meaning of 'similar'—

sañjanā	*ramāyāḥ*	*sadṛśī*	*asti.*
Sanjana	Rama	like	is
prath.sing.	ṣaṣṭhī sing.	adj.	be verb pres.3rd pers. sing.

Sanjana resembles Rama.

For standing out of many, ṣaṣṭhī is used optionally—

kavīnām/kaviṣu	*kālidāsaḥ*	*śreṣṭhaḥ.*
Poets	Kalidas	great
ṣaṣ./sapt.plural	nom.sing.	adj. sing.

Kalidas is greatest among poets.

For indicating love or affection—

(i)	*prakṛtyaiva*	*priyā*	*sītā*	*rāmasya*	*āsīt.*
	By nature	dear	Sita	Ram	be
	tri.sing. stress indec.	adj.fem.	noun nom.	ṣaṣṭhī	ver. pas. sing.

Naturally Sita was dear to Ram.

(ii)	*kāyaḥ*	*kasya*	*na*	*vallabhaḥ.*
	Body	who	not	dear
	prath. sing.	ṣaṣṭhī poss. pro.sing.	neg. parti.	adj.sing.

Who does not love his/her body.

For a causative situation—

adhyayanasya hetoḥ sā amerikādeśe nivasati.

Study	reason	she	America	live
(ṣaṣṭhī)	ṣaṣṭhī	pron.	sapta.sing.	ver.
noun		fem. nom. sing.		pres3rd pers.sing.

She is living in America for study.

For words like upari (above), agre (before,in front), paścāt (behind), adhaḥ (below)—

bhavatām	*agre*	*prastaumi.*
You	before	present
pro.ṣaṣṭh.plu.	indec.	ver.pres.1st.per.sing. no.

I present before you.

Genitive is used for Dative like situation—

Ko'tibhāraḥ	*samarthānām.*
What too heavy	vigorous
ques.indec.adj.nom.sing.	genit. Plu.

What is too heavy for the vigorous.

kim	*krūram*	*vyavasāyinām.*
What	dangerous	audacious
quest.	adj.nom.neu.	genit.plur.

What is dangerous for the audacious.

7. Locative Case (Saptamī Vibhakti)—

In the structure of a sentence, locative case hints at the locality, base of the action; where the action is taking place. The examples are—

(i)

kakśāyām	*chạ̄trāḥ*	*pathanti.*
Class	students	study
loc.sing.	nom.plur.	ver. pres.pro.plur.

Students are studying in the class.

(ii)

mātā	*sthālyām*	*bhojanam*	*pacati.*
Mother	pot	food	cook
nom.	loc.sing.	obj.dvit.sing.	ver.pres.

Mother cooks food in the pot.

(iii)	*tileṣu*	*tailam*	*asti.*
	Sesamum	oil	be
	loc.plur.	nom.neut.sing.	ver. pres. sing.

There is oil in the sesamum seeds.

(iv)	*tasya*	*adhyayane*	*ruciḥ.*
	He	study	interest
	pron.geni. sing.	noun loc. sing.	noun nom. sing.

He has interest in study.

Locative Case is used for displaying affection—

(i)	*śakuntalāyām*	*anuraktaḥ*	*duṣyantaḥ.*
	Shakutala	in love	Dushyanta
	noun loc. sing.	adj.nom. sing.	nom. sing.

Dushyanta is in love with Shakuntala.

(ii)	*katham*	*bālye`smin*	*snihyati*	*me*	*manaḥ.*
	Why	child this	affection	I	heart
	ques. indec.	noun pro. loc.sing.	ver. pres. 3rd pers.sing.	pro.geni sing.	noun mas.

Why my heart goes out for this child.

For indicating cause—

carmaṇi	*dvīpinam*	*hanti*
Skin	tiger	kill
noun loc. sing.	noun dvitī. sing.	ver. pres. 3rd pers.sing.

(he) kills tiger for skin.

dantayoḥ	*hanti*	*kuñjaram.*
Teeth	kill	elephant
noun loc.dual	ver.pres.sing.	obj.dvi.sing.

(He) kills elephant for teeth.

The effect is put in locative case when 'cause' is indicated—

daivameva	*hi*	*nṛṇām*	*vṛddhau*	*kśhaye*
Fate	inde.	man	prosperity	decline
noun inde.		noun	noun fem.	noun
neu. nom.		gen.plu.	loc. sing.	mas.loc. sing.

kāraṇam.
cause
nom. sing.

Fate alone is the cause of prosperity and decline of men.

For indicating the circumstances under which an action is taking place—

rudati	*śiśau*	*mātā*	*gatā.*
Weep	child	mother	go
ver.part.	noun loc.	noun nom.	ver. pas. part.
loc.sing.	sing.	sing.	sing.

Mother went while the child was crying.

sūryāste	*rādhā*	*gṛham*	*pratyāgacchat.*
Sunset	Radha	house	come.
noun loc.	noun nom.	obj. dvi.	ver.with prep.
sing.	sing.	sing.	pas.sing.

Radha came home after the sunset.

For words like **'pravīṇaḥ, kuśalaḥ'** etc. indicating skill—

pradīpaḥ	*mṛdaṅgavādane*	*pravīṇaḥ*	*asti.*
Pradipa	drum play	skill	be
noun nom.	noun loc.sing.	adj.nom.	ver.sing.
		sing.	pres.sing.

Pradipa is skilled in playing mridang (drum).

For using words like 'yukta' (proper), niyukta (engaged) etc.—

	yuktarūpam	*idam*	*tvayi.*
(i)	Fit	this	you
	neut.nom.sing.	neu.nom.sing.	pron. loc. sing.

This is fit for you.

(ii)	*saḥ*	*niyuktaḥ*	*kampyūṭaravidyāyām.*
	He	engage	computer
	pron. mas. nom.sing.	ver.part.	noun. loc.sing.

He is engaged in computer learning.

For indicating 'good' or 'bad'—

mātari	*sādhuḥ/asādhuḥ.*
Mother	good/bad
noun loc.sing.	noun mas. sing.

(He) is good/bad towards his mother.

For using verbs like **muc, kśip, nyas** etc.—

(i)	*mṛgeṣu*	*śarān*	*mumoca.*
	Deer	arrow	throw
	noun mas. loc.plu.	noun neu.dvi.plu.	ver.pas. sing.

(he) threw arrows on deer.

saciveṣu	*rājyabhāraḥ*	*nyastaḥ.*
Minister	duties of government	place
noun mas. loc.plu.	noun mas.nom. sing.	ver.pas.part.sing.

(He) placed upon the ministers the duties of the government.

With words like **prasita, utsuka** in the meaning of 'very desirous' Locative is used optionally with Instrumental Case—

sudhīraḥ	*gamane/gamanena*	*utsukaḥ*	*asti.*
Sudhira	go	desirious	be
noun mas. nom.	noun neu.loc./inst. sing.	noun mas.nom.	ver. pres. sing.

Sudhira is longing to go.

With root 'rādh' with 'apa' indeclinable in the meaning of 'offend'—

kasminnapi	*pūjārhe*	*aparāddhā*	*śakuntalā.*
Someone	respectable	offend	Shakuntala
pro.loc.sing.	adj. mas. loc.sing.	adj. fem. nom.sing.	nom.sing.

Shakuntala has offended someone respectable.

8. Vocative Case (Sambodhana)—

Vocative Case is used for addressing or calling someone. In Sanskrit it is known as **sambodhana kāraka**. It is designed in **prathamā vibhakti** without visarga in singular number in masculine gender. The particles used for this are 'he, aho' etc.—

he kṛṣṇa	*tvam*	*mama*	*śaraṇam.*
O Krishna!	you	I	shelter
noun voc.	pro.nom. sing.	pro.gen. sing.	noun neu. nom.sing.

O Krishna! I am in your control.

Case endings—

The case-ending in Sanskrit depends on the gender and category of the stem, the stem having a different gender will have a different case-ending. Sanskrit words are classified in three numbers— singular, dual and plural. The dual number in Nominative takes vṛddhi, provided the word ends with a vowel; **rāmau, gurū, harī.**

Nominative Case—

In Nominative case in masculine gender **'a'** ending stems have **s** in singular form, stems in feminine (ā or ī ending) do not have s and stems in neuter gender ending with **a** have **am**. Words ending in other vowels remain the same. The dual takes vṛddhi, depending on the end vowel; rāmau, gurū, harī. In plural masculine, ending with **a** the word takes vṛddhi— **ās**, but when it ends in **i** or **u** vowels, it takes **ayas** and **avas** respectively.

Accusative Case—

In Accusative, words in masculine gender take **am,** in feminine ām, īm depending on the end vowel and in neuter gender it takes the nominative sign in singular number. Dual is same as in nominative case. In plural **a** ending stem takes **ān** in masculine, words in feminine and neuter remain same as in nominative case.

Instrumental Case—

The case ending in Instrumental case is **ā**, which is combined differently with different stems. In masculine and neuter singular it becomes **ena,** in feminine it is **ayā.** In dual, in masculine, feminine and neuter the case ending becomes bhyām. In plural number **a** ending stem in masculine and neuter gender becomes **eiḥ,** stems ending in other vowels in masculine and feminine generally, take **bhiḥ**.

Dative Case—

Here the case ending is **e.** With masculine singular **a** ending stem takes **āya,** the feminine takes **yai**.

Ablative Case—

The case ending here is **t/d.** With masculine singular **a** ending stem takes **āt**, neuter takes the same. Other vowel ending stems take the same case ending in Ablative and Genitive case, depending on the end- vowel of the stem. In feminine too, the Ablative and Genitive singular becomes **āyāḥ** or **yāḥ.** In plural in masculine, feminine and neuter, the ending becomes **bhyaḥ** in Dative and Ablative both.

Genitive Case—

In masculine singular, the case ending is **sya**, the feminine takes same case– ending as Ablative. For masculine and feminine plural, the case– ending is **nām.** Dual generally takes yoḥ.

Locative Case—

In locative, the case ending is **e.** In masculine singular **a** ending stem takes **e** and in plural it takes **eṣu,** in rest the end- vowel becomes **vṛddhi; gurau**, **harau**. In feminine it takes **ām** for singular and **āsu** or **iṣu** in plural. Dual takes the same as in Genitive Case.

V.2

Case in Manipuri

Manipuri grammarians have varied opinion about the number of Cases. Early grammarians limited the number to five or six. Kalachand Shastri (1960) recognized six cases, he did not include Genitive and Vocative. Nandlal Sharma (1965) and Dwijamani Dev Sharma (1969) acknowledged seven Cases, they included Vocative Case also. Thoudam (1996) declared Nominative, Accusative, Instrumental, Genitive, Particularisation and Locative Cases. Bhat and Ningomba (1997) discussed five primary case suffixes; Nominative, accusative, Locative, Genitive and Connective as primary cases and they treated Dative, Instrumental, and Ablative as the extended forms of the primary Cases. Ch. Yashawanta Singh (2000) has discussed eight Cases, he has not included Dative, instead he has included Associative Case. Thus with this additional Case, the number of Cases matched with the number in Sanskrit Grammar. Another linguist Mr. Sharatchandra (2000) went a step further; he included Benefactive and Connective Case which is accepted as Associative Case elsewhere, hence determining the number of nine Cases.

1. Nominative Case—

The Nominative Case is used to indicate the doer or agent of the action as in Sanskrit. The case marker is– **'na'** which is not obligatory; it may be used, it may not be. The examples are—

1. *tomba (na)* *cāk* *cāri.*

   Tomba nom. food accus. eat asp.

   Tomba is eating food.

2. *mahāk (na)* *catli.*

He/she nom. go asp.

He/she is going.

In certain condition use of '**na**' marker becomes imminent—

(i) When 'bu' is not used for Accusative Case; for example—

manoj na *anju* *phui.*

Manoj nom. Anju accus. beat asp.

Manoj beat Anju.

(ii) When the subject is being specified; for example—

raghu na *leirik* *pāri.*

Raghu nom. book accus. read asp.

Raghu is reading the book.

Here in the above sentence, the meaning is that Rghu is reading, others are not; similarly,

radha na	*jagoy*	*sāri*	*mirā na*	*isay*	*sakli.*
Radha nom.	dance accus.	perform asp.	Meera nom.	song accus.	sing asp.

Radha is dancing, Meera is singing.

Here in the second sentence it is specified that Radha is dancing and Meera is singing, not Meera dancing and Radha singing.

2. Accusative Case—

Accusative Case is used for the object in a sentence, **'bu/pu'** is the case marker in this case. It is not essential to use the marker but its use is common in Manipuri, for example—

(i) *mamā na* *aṅgāṅg (bu)* *caire.*

Mother nom. child accus. beat asp.

Mother beats child.

(ii)	*ojhā na*	*saritā (bu)*	*khaṅgī.*
	teacher nom.	Sarita accus.	know asp.

The teacher knows Sarita.

Use of both types of sentences is common in Manipuri language, but the use of '**bu**' makes the object more specific.

- In Manipuri, the Accusative Casc is applied for two types of objects— direct object and indirect object, but the marker is used with the indirect object; not with direct object, for·example—

mamā na	*rāni bu*	*paisā*	*pī.*
Mother nom.	Rani accus ind.	money accus dir.	give asp.

Mother gives money to Rani.

- Traditional grammarians have recommended use of '**bu**' with direct (inanimate) object also, when the situation is specified; the example is—

naṅ na	*nāpi bu*	*asuk*	*tāthīrība,*	*karīgīnw?*
you nom.	grass accus.	much adj.	illtreat asp	why interj.

Why are you so cruel to grass.

Accusative marker is also found in use in the form of '**causing to**', for example—

(i)	*ojhā na*	*ranjit bu*	*layrik*	*pāhalle.*
	Teacher nom.	Ranjit accus.	book accus.	make read asp. causative.

Teacher made Rajit read the book.

(ii)	*indomcā na*	*radha bu*	*cāk*	*thoṅhalle.*
	Aunty nom.	Radha accu.	food accu.	make cook asp. causative.

Aunty made Radha cook food.

'**Bu**' also occurs in the passive meaning with indirect object—

sānti bu *kolej da* *ojhā* *hāple.*

Santi accu (ind. object)	college loc.	teacher accu.	appoint asp. (passive).

Santi has been appointed as a teacher in the college.

(ii)	*rājiv bu*	*chairman*	*khanle.*
	Rajiv accus. (ind. object)	chairman accus.	elected asp passive.

Rajiv has been appointed as chairman.

3. Instrumental Case—

The medium or the tool used by the doer for his action is determined in Instrumental Case and it takes '**na**' marker—

(i)	*ramā*	*kolom na*	*ciṭṭhi*	*iri.*
	Rama nom.	pen instr.	letter accus.	write asp.

Rama is writing letter with pen.

(ii)	*dharmendra*	*kār na*	*skūl*	*catle.*
	Dharmendra nom.	car instr.	school loc.	go asp.

Dharmendra went to school by car.

(iii)	*ranjit na*	*aṅgāṅgba*	*macu na*	*citra*	*amā*	*sāy.*
	Ranji nom.	red	colour instr.	picture accus.	one	make asp.

Ranjit made a picture with red colour.

- Instrumental Case is also used to show the cause of mental or physical condition, for example—

(i)	*samīr*	*leihau na*	*nāri.*
	Sameer nom.	fever instr.	ill asp.

Sameer is ill with fever.

(ii)	*lilā gi mi na*	*lilā na*	*marol*	*lolli.*
	actor nom.	acting instr.	language accus.	speak asp.

Actor speaks through his/her acting.

- '**Na**'marker can precede '**bu**' in a situation when contrast or contrary to the expectation is indicated and '**ga**' when exclusiveness is shown, for example—

(i)	*mahāk*	*kāti na bu*	*koi*	*kakki.*
	He	scissors	beard	shave
	nom.	instr contr.	accus.	asp.

He shaves his beard with scissors.

This implies that he should have shaved his beard with blade instead of scissors.

(ii)	*prasād*	*pencil ga na*	*ī.*
	Prasad nom.	pencil instr.excl.	write asp.

Prasad writes with pencil (only).

(iii)	*sanjay*	*cycle na ga*	*imphal*	*catle.*
	Sanjay	cycle	Imphal	Catle
	nom.	instr. excl.	loc.	go asp.

Sanjay goes to Imphal on cycle.

4. Dative Case—

In Manipuri, the Dative Case is used to indicate the beneficiary, the marker for this is '**da**'—

(i)	*babā na*	*cānu da*	*paisā*	*pīre.*
	Father nom.	Chanu dat.	money accus.	give asp.

Father gave money to Chanu.

(ii)	*phurit asi*	*aṅgāṅ da*	*chilli.*
	Shirt this nom.	child dat.	tight asp.

This shirt is tight for the child.

- Dative Case is also used to indicate the possessor—

ayṅgonda	*tagore gi*	*leirik amā*	*lay.*
I dat.	Tagore gen.	book accus.	is simple asp.

I have Tagore's book.

* Use of '**da**' is obligatory in a sentence where feeding of a person or an animal is involved, for example—

With '**da**'

(i) *mamā na* *macā da* *saṅgom* *pithaye.*
Mother nom. child dat. milk accu. feed asp.

Mother fed milk to child.

(ii) *pushpā na* *hui da* *roṭi* *ille.*
Pushpa nom. dog dat. bread accus. feed asp.

Pushpa fed bread to the dog.

Without '**da**'

(i) *mamā na macā saṅgom pithaye.*

(ii) pushpa na hui roti ille.

Both the usages are grammatically correct, in both the sentences direct feeding is involved.

5. Locative Case—

Locative Case indicates place or location of action, 'da' marker is used in this case also—

(i) *sāmo* *cauki da* *phammī.*
Samo nom. chair loc. sit asp.

Samo is sitting on the chair.

(ii) *sarita* *cākhum da* *lay.*
Sarita nom. kitchen loc. is asp. simple.

Sarita is in the kitchen.

- However, use of '**da**' becomes optional if predicate indicating direction, movement is used in a sentence—

(i) *nakāto* *thoubal da* *chatkhre.*
Or
nakāto *thoubal* *chatkhre.*
Nakato nom. Thoubal loc. go asp. perf.

Nakato has gone to Thoubal.

- *san* *skūl da* *caṅghre.*
Or

san *skūl* *caṅghre.*
Cow nom school loc. enter. asp. perf.

Cow has entered the school.

- Use of '**da**' is also optional with adverb of time—

(i) *rājīv* *ahiṅ da* *yum* *halay.*

Or

rajiv *ahiṅ* *yum* *halay.*
Rajiv nom. night loc. home loc. return asp.

Rajiv returned home in the night.

(ii) *priyā* *ayuk da* *leirik* *pāri.*

Or

priyā *ayuk* *leirik* *pāri.*
Priya nom. morning loc. book accus. read asp.

Priya reads book in the morning.

- The Locative marker may or may not be used with certain post-positions; **mathak** –on/ upon, **manuṅ**—inside, **mapān**—outside. The examples are—

(i) *kā manuṅ da* *lī* *lay.*

Or

kā manuṅ *lī* *lay.*
Room inside loc. snake nom. is asp.

Snake is inside the room.

(ii) *chātra* *skūl mapān da* *thokhre.*

Or

chātra skūl mapān thokhre.
Student school outside go
nom. post-position loc. asp perf.

The student has gone outside school.

- '**Da**' marker is used in a situation where time is mentioned; for example—

(i) *indira* *puṅ tarā da* *office* *catle.*

Indira	ten o' clock	office	go
nom.	loc.	loc.	asp. simple.

Indira goes to office at ten o' clock.

(ii) *ramesh*	*noṅgmāyjiṅ da*	*skūl*	*catloy.*
Ramesh	Sunday	school	go neg.
nom.	loc.	loc.	asp. unrealized.

Ramesh will not go to school on Sunday.

- The meaning of a sentence becomes different with the use of **'da'** while indicating 'time'—

(i) *sanjay*	*puṅ amā da*	*leirik*	*pāre.*
Sanjay nom.	one o' clock loc.	book accus.	read asp.

Sanjay read book at one o' clock.

(ii) *binodini*	*noṅgmā da*	*dilli*	*halay.*
Binodini nom.	one day loc.	Delhi loc.	return asp.

Binodini returned to Delhi in one day.

Without '**da**'

(i) *sanjay*	*puṅ amā*	*leirik*	*pāre.*
Sanjay nom.	one hour loc.	book	read asp.

Sanjay read book for one hour.

(iii) *Binodini*	*noṅmā*	*dilli*	*halay.*
Binodini nom.	one day loc.	Delhi loc.	return asp.

Binodini returned to Delhi one day.

- Cause is also indicated by locative case—

ranjit	*leirik*	*kanna pāba da*	*first*	*tāre.*
Rnjit	book	hard study	first	stand
nom.	accus.	cause NZR loc.	adj.	asp.

Ranjit stood first due to hard study.

- Locative Case is also used for indicating possession—

miṅgon da	*aygi*	*leirik*	*lay.*
He/she loc.	I gen.	book accus.	is asp. simple.

He/she possesses my book.

6. Ablative case –

Ablative Case deals with the source of separation, expulsion, **'dagi/tagi'** marker is used in this case, for example—

(i) *rājkumār* *office dagi* *halay.*
Rajkumar nom. office abl. return asp perf.

Rajkumar returned from the office.

(ii) *haynaw* *ū dagi* *kelli.*
Mango nom. tree abl. fall asp perf.

Mango fell from the tree.

(iii) *romi na* *vīnā dagi* *bag* *laure.*
Romi nom. Veena abl. bag accus. take asp perf.

Romi took bag from Veena.

- Ablative Case is also used to indicate the source of a thing—

haṅgām dagi *thāu* *summī.*
Mustard abl. oil nom. extract asp.

Oil is extracted from mustard.

- **'Dagi'** marker also indicates cause—

ronit *theṅgba dagi* *lākte.*
Ronit nom. late cause abl. come negative asp.

Ronit did not come because he got late.

- Ablative marker is also used to indicate the comparison between two persons or more—

(i) *shilā dagi* *ramā* *henna* *wāṅ ṅī.*
Shila abl. Rama nom. more comp. tall adj is asp.

Rama is taller than Shila.

(iii) *hay* *mithāi dagi* *phay hele.*
Fruit nom. sweetmeat abl. comp. better adj is asp.

Fruit is better than sweetmeat.

7. Genitive Case—

Genitive Case shows the relationship between two substantives, the latter of the two is the agent and **'gi'** is the case- marker; for example—

(i)	*rādhesyām*	*punit gi*	*mapā ni.*
	Radhesyam nom.	Punit gen.	father be asp.

Radhesyam is Punit's father.

(ii)	*pinki gi*	*mamā*	*keithel*	*catli.*
	Pinki gen.	mother nom.	market loc.	go asp.

Pinki's mother went to market.

- Genitive case can also be used to indicate the beneficiary of action—

(i)	*masi phurit*	*sanāmacā gi*	*nī.*
	This shirt nom.	Sanamaca gen.	be asp.

This shirt is for Sanamaca.

(iv)	*rājan na*	*si chātin*	*tanu gi*	*lay.*
	Rajan nom.	this umbrella accus.	Tanu gen.	buy asp.

Rajan bought this umbrella for Tanu.

- This **'gi'** marker is also used to show the purpose of action, in that case it is followed by **'damak'** marker—

(i)	*layrik tamba gi damak*	*sofiā*	*hostel da*	*lay.*
	Study gen. purpose	Sofia nom.	hostel loc.	stay asp.

Sofia is staying in the hostel for study purpose.

(ii)	*tamphāsanā*	*business gi damak*	*u k*	*catle.*
	Tamphasana nom.	business geni. purpose	UK loc.	go asp.

Tamphasana went to UK for business purpose.

These types of usages have been discussed separately in Benefactive Case by some scholars, whereas these have been included in Genitive Case by others.

8. Associative Case—

In Manipuri language a sentence takes Associative Case when an action is performed in association with other person or persons, for this **'ga'** marker is used—

(i) *sandhyā* *syāmā ga* *skūl* *catli.*
Sandhya nom. Syama asso. school loc. go asp.
Sandhya goes to school with Syama.

(ii) *bunti* *mamānabā ga* *sānari.*
Bunti nom. friend asso. play asp. simple.
Bunti is playing with his friend.

- **'Ga'** marker can also indicate exchange of argument, fight with a person—

(i) *rajni* *lila ga* *khannari.*
Rajni nom. Lila asso. argue asp. simple.
Rajni is arguing with Lila.

(ii) *pintu* *rubi ga* *phūnari.*
Pintu nom. Rubi asso. fight.
Pintu is fighting with Rubi.

- **'Ga'** is also used with Accusative Case indicating along with—

bhānu na *thāu ga* *sāpon amā* *lam na* *phaṅṅī.*
Bhanu nom. oil asso. soap accus. free get asp.
Bhanu got a free soap with oil.

- **'Ga'** marker can also be used with two successive NPs—

rādheshyām ga *rājen ga* *dillī* *catkhre.*
Radheshyam ass. Rajen con. NP Delhi loc. go asp perf.
Radheshyam and Rajen have gone to Delhi.

9. Vocative Case—

This case is used for calling or addressing a person,

the case affixes are O, he, ho, ha. These affixes are also seen omitted while addressing. Word 'sā' is used to indicate plural number—

(i) *O ibuṅgo,*	*sida*	*lāo.*
O son voc.	here loc.	come asp. command.

O son, come here.

(ii) *O aṅgāṅgsā,*	*nakhoy gi*	*yum*	*catlo.*
O children	you	home	go asp
voc.	gen.	loc.	command.

O children, go to your home.

* When a person is addressed, then the last vowel is lengthened—

imā...,	*cāk*	*pībīro.*
Mother... voc.	food (rice)	give asp request.

Mother, please give food.

Double Case -Marking—

In Manipuri language the use of double case- marking is a very common feature. In such situation first case–marker with the noun is the real case- marker and the second one succeeding the first marker is used to stress the pragmatic significance. Generally, the second case-marker attached to the previous one , loses its property to imply the specific meaning. The latter marker is called a 'clitic', this marker can imply emphasis, exclusiveness, contrary to expectation etc.

The frequently and commonly used 'clitics' are **na, bu, ga**, these can be attached to any case- marker except itself. For example, **na** cannot take **na** as the preceding marker, similarly **bu** and **ga** can not take the same marker. The Ablative **dagi** marker gives a false impression of consisting double case-marker— **da** (locative) and **gi** (genitive) but it has not been accepted by linguists as a double case-marker and it remains as an Ablative case- marker only. Below is given a list of double case-markers—

1. **na** as a second marker—

(i) 'bu na'—

ojhā na	*tomba bu na*	*yāmna*	*cayre.*
Teacher nom.	Tomba accus.	much excess	scold asp.

Teacher scolded Tomba a lot (not others).

(ii) 'da na'—

mapā na	*bābu da na*	*lupā kun*	*pī.*
Father nom.	Babu dat.	Rs. twenty accus.	give asp.

Father gave Rs. twenty to Babu (not others).

(iii) 'da na'—

aṅgāṅ	*leibāk da na*	*tummī.*
Child nom.	floor loc.	sleep asp.

Child is sleeping on the floor (not on bed).

(iv) 'ga na'—

ranjitā	*ramā ga na*	*skūl*	*catli.*
Ranjita nom.	Rama asso.	school loc.	go asp.

Ranjita goes to school with Rama (only).

(v) 'gi na'—

tāmo na	*suresh gi na*	*phi*	*lay.*
Brother nom.	Suresh gen. benef.excl.	cloth accus.	buy asp.

Brother bought clothes for Suresh (only).

(vi) 'dagi na'—

rāni	*thoubal dagi na*	*kihom*	*pāme.*
Rani nom.	Thoubal abl.	pineapple accus.	like asp.

Rani likes Pineapple from Thoubal.

2. **'bu'** as a second marker—

(i) 'na bu'—

mahāk na bu	*kari*	*tauganī.*
He nom.	what inte.	do asp. future.

What will he do? (implying 'he will not do anything)

Such combination indicates an unthinkable situation.

(ii) 'na bu'—

sarojini na	*pencil na bu*	*ciṭṭhī*	*ire.*
Sarojini nom.	pencil instr.	letter accus.	write asp.

Sarojini wrote the letter with pencil (whereas she should have written in pen.)

(iii) 'da bu'—

mamā na	*rāgini da bu*	*lupā cā maṅgā*	*pīre.*
Mother nom.	Ragini dat.	Rs. 500 accus.	give asp.

Mother gave Ragini Rs. 500. (she should not have given.)

(iv) 'da bu'—

bābulāl	*agra da bu*	*yāore/layre..*
Babulal nom.	Agra loc.	stay asp.

Babulal stayed at Agra. (he should not have stayed there.)

(v) 'ga bu'—

nikitā na	*sanā ga bu*	*layrik*	*pāri.*
Nikita nom.	Sana asso.	book accu.	read.

Nikita studies along with Sana. (she should study with some other girl.)

(vi) 'gi bu'—

santā	*rājen gi bu*	*khalli.*
Santa nom.	Rajen ben.	think asp.

Santa thinks only for Rajen. (not for others.)

(vii) 'dagi bu'—

Bablu	*chauki dagi bu*	*tāre.*
Bablu nom.	chair abl.	fall asp.

Bablu fell from the chair. (he should not have fallen)

3. '**ga**' as second marker—

(i) 'na ga'—

manju da	*babā na ga*	*paisa*	*pī.*
Manju dat.	father nom. incl.	money accus.	give asp.

Father (also) gave money to Manju.

(ii) 'na ga'—

ronit	*oy khud na ga*	*sānare.*
Ronit nom.	left hand instr. incl.	play asp.

Ronit plays with left hand as well.

(iii) 'bu ga'—

Reshmā na	*pammi bu ga*	*puray.*
Reshma nom.	Pammi accus.	bring asp.

Reshma brought Pammi as well.

(iv) 'da ga'—

sandip na	*ranjan da ga*	*leirik*	*pīre.*
Sandip nom.	Ranjan dat.incl.	book accus.	give asp.

Sandip gave book to Ranjan as well.

(v) 'da ga'—

aṅgāṅ na	*nuṅthin da ga*	*tumme.*
Child nom.	afternoon loc. adv.	sleep asp.

Child sleeps in the afternoon as well.

(vi) 'gi ga'—

sanjanā na	*punita gi ga*	*shawl*	*lay.*
Sanjana nom.	Punita bene.incl.	shawl accu.	buy asp.

Sanjana bought shawl for Punita as well.

(vii) 'dagi ga'—

tāmo na	*ambala dagi ga*	*suitcase*	*lay.*
Brother nom.	Ambala abl.incl.	suitcase accu.	buy asp.

Brother bought suitcase from Ambala as well.

Double case– marker **'gi da'** is often used, here both markers represent their respective meanings— genitive as well as locative, for example;

Memā	*ṅgarāṅ*	*aykhoy gi da*	*lāye*
Mema nom.	yesterday adv.	we gen. loc.	come asp.

Mema came to our house yesterday.

There is also a practice of using two 'clitics' to a marker which is already attached with a noun or a pronoun, such as—

(i) 'da na bu'—

After the case-marker **'da'** which indicates Dative Case, insertion of **'na bu'** combination implies exclusiveness, the position of these clitics may be vice-vera—**da bu na.**

(ii) 'ga na bu'—

Here '**ga**' is indicating Associative Case and **'na bu'** are used as clitics.

Here too, it hints at the stress or exclusiveness, this can also be used as '**ga bu na**'.

Similarly, '**gi na bu**'also expresses the same meaning and this combination of clitics can also be used as '**gi bu na.**

Case-Roles with different Meaning—

A sentence constructed with two different case-roles may seem to denote the same meaning, but by close observation we can identify the difference, for example—

tilhau	*thāṅ na*	*kakku.*
Onion accu.	knife inst.	cut asp. command.

Cut onion with knife.

And

tilahu	*thāṅ da*	*kakku.*
Onion accus.	knife loc.	cut asp. command.

Cut onion with knife.

Here with the use of Instrumental Case-Role the meaning is implied that the knife is at one's approach and he/she should cut the onion with that.

With the use of Locative Case-Role it implies that he/she should fetch the knife and cut the onion, the knife is at some distance.

Conclusion

Accusative Case—

There is a provision in Sanskrit that a sentence can take two objects (Accusatives), we come across this system in Manipuri also.

In different situations in Sanskrit the sentence demands Accusative case-marker instead of other case- markers. In Manipuri, according to the situation, the bu marker can be added to other case- markers also. The difference is that in Sanskrit in this situation the Accusative marker works independently for other cases, whereas in Manipuri it goes along with other case- markers; here it is used only for specificity, for example—

Manipuri:	*aṅgāṅ*	*na bu*	*saṅgom*	*pāmde.*
	Child	nom.	milk accus.	like not asp.

Child does not like milk.

With Nominative case-marker—to specify

mamā na	*aṅgāṅ*	*da bu*	*cāk*	*pīde.*
Mother nom.	child	dat.	food accus.	give not asp.

Mother did not give food to the child. (It indicates that she should have given).

Sometimes this marker is used to indicate the adversative situation or contrary to expectation—

Damo na	*isiṅ bu*	*haidoe.*
Damo nom.	water advers.	Throw asp.

Damo spilled water. (He should not have spilled water).

Sanskrit:

1.	*gurutvam*	*naram*	*nayanti.*
	Respectability accus.	man accus.	bring pres.

In place of Dative

They take man to respectability.

2. *saḥ* *taṇḍulān* *odanam* *pacati.*
He nom. rice accus. pulao accus. cook pres.

In place of Instrumental

He cooks pulao from rice.

3. *radha* *vṛkśam* *puṣpam* *cinoti.*
Radha nom. tree accus. flower accus. pluck pres.

In place of Ablative

Radha plucks flower from the tree.

Instrumental Case—

In Sanskrit Instrumental Case is used if the characteristics or nature (guṇa) becomes the cause of action—

1. *saḥ* *jāḍyena* *baddhaḥ.*
He nom. foolishness instr. catch verb past partic.

He was caught because of his foolishness.

2. *duryodhanaḥ* *svabhāvena* *krūraḥ* *āsīt.*
Duryodhana nom. nature instr. cruel was be verb past.

Duryodhan was cruel by nature.

We find this application in Manipuri language also—

mahāk *layhāu na* *nāri.*
He/ she nom. fever instr. ill asp.

He/ she is down with fever.

Dative Case—

Sanskrit has great many varied situations where Dative Case is used, including beneficiary of action; for example—

1. *nṛpaḥ* *yācakāya* *dhanam* *dadāti.*
King nom. beggar dat. alms accus. give verb pres.

King gives alms to the beggar.

2.	*mahyam*	*jalam*	*ānaya.*
	I dat.	water accus.	bring verb imper.

Bring water for me.

Beneficiary takes Dative Case in Manipuri also—

mamā	*añyūṅ da*	*paisa*	*pīri.*
Mother nom.	child dat.	money accus.	give asp. Simple.

Mother gives money to the child.

Possessor does not take Dative in Sanskrit as it takes in Manipuri—

Sanskrit:	*idam*	*pustakam*	*mama*	*samīpe*	*asti.*
	This	book nom.	I genet.	Near prepo.	Is be verb pres.

This book is with me.

Manipuri:	*ayṅgonda*	*si layrik*	*lai.*
	I dat.	this book	is asp.

This book is with me.

Locative Case—

Locative Case is used to indicate the base or place of action in both the languages, this includes time also. In Manipuri it is used to show the reason—

mahāk	*nāba da*	*office*	*lākte.*
He nom.	ill health loc.	office loc.	come neg. asp.

He did not come to the office due to ill health.

We find such uses in Sanskrit also—

carmaṇi	*dvīpinam*	*hanti*	*dantayor*	*hanti*	*kuñjaram.*
Skin loc.	tiger accus.	kill pres.	tusk loc.	kill	elephant accus.

He kills tiger for skin and elephant for tusks.

Here skin and tusks become the reason for killing.

Associative Case—

Manipuri language includes Associative as a case in case- category, where as in Sanskrit language this case is included in Instrumental Case only; in such situation saha marker is used with the associative person or persons—

rāmeṇa	*saha*	*sītā*	*vanam*	*agamat.*
Rama	marker	Sita	forest	go past
instr.		nom.	accus.	pref.

Sita went to forst with Rama.

For **Vocative Case** the pattern is the same in both the languages, affixes are used. In address the last vowel is lengthened.

In Sanskrit there is a rule defying all the rules regarding case-positions—vivakśātaḥ kārakāṇi bhavanti (Case depends on the desire of the speaker). Pāṇini has written specific rules for putting various case-markers according to the situation in a syntax but if the speaker wishes to put a certain syntactical unit in a certain case- role, he is allowed to do so. Different case-roles can take the role of an agent (kartā) if the situation demands—

kabīraḥ	*kāṣṭṭhai*	*sthālyām*	*bhojanam*	*pacati.*
Kabir	wood	cooker	food	cook
nom.	instr.	loc.	accus.	pres.

Kabir is cooking food in a cooker with wooden sticks.

*If wooden sticks are burning nicely and helping cooking fast then the Instrumental Case (wooden sticks) take the role of agent and the sentence becomes 'kāṣṭṭhāni bhojanam pacanti.'

* If the cooker is of good quality and does not take long in cooking food, in that situation also word **sthālī** which was in Locative Case originally, will become the agent itself and the sentence will be 'sthālī bhojanam pacati'.

VI.1

Compound in Sanskrit

A compound word consists of two or more words which joined together give a complete and single expression. The words in a compound may not have a relation between them independently, but as a whole, the compound indicates various relations which exist between the component parts. A compound has the ability to be compounded again with a simple or a compound word and further again. In Sanskrit, we have the tradition of compound words, whether they are simple words, verbs or indeclinables, adjectives or substantives. This trend is found in Indo-European languages also but the enormous development in this syntactical aspect is the characteristic feature of Sanskrit language only. In J. S. Speijer's words, "there exists in that language (Sanskrit) an almost unlimited freedom of expressing any kind of relations, grammatical or logical, by the way of compounding." (Sanskrit Syntax pg.146). In Vedic literature, the compound words are mostly formed of two stems but in the later literature, with time the trend started with more than two stems. It was considered a beauty of the literature having difficult and complex compounds.

In a compound in Sanskrit, the last word requires the case termination and rest of the words remain in their crude form; for example— rājan puruṣaḥ = rājapuruṣaḥ (a royal man), vidvas + janaḥ = vidvajjanaḥ (a learned person). The change in the final vowel or consonant of preceding component of a compound, while being joined with the succeeding components, follows the usual rules of the sandhi.

In certain cases, the preceding members retain their

case-endings, this type of compounds are **'aluk'**; for example— sarasijam = a lotus, yudhiṣṭhiraḥ = the name of the eldest Pāṇḍava. In both these compounds, the locative case is retained in the preceding component; saras (anything flowing) and yudh (battle).

Generally, a vigrahavākya (the expounding of a compound) expresses the relation existing between the objects indicated by various components in a compound, but sometimes a vigrahavākya can not be given of a compound; in such situation the compound is known as **nityasamāsa**.

The feminine indicator in the primary elements in a compound is retained in a situation when feminine is treated as a formal name or a title. In case its sign is omitted, the compound may lose its very meaning— kalyāṇīmātā = mother of a beautiful girl; here in this compound the feminine indicator in the preceding element' kalyāṇī' is retained. If the feminine is used as a mere predicate, the feminine suffix may be dropped; śobhanabhāryaḥ = one who has a beautiful wife; here the feminine suffix in the preceding component śobhana is dropped because the compound ending is in masculine gender.

In Sanskrit compound has been divided into four categories: 1. Tatpuruṣa or Determinative 2. Dwandwa or Copulative 3. Bahuvrīhi or Attributive 4. Avyayībhāva or Adverbial.

1. Tatpuruṣa or Determinative— In a Tatpuruṣa compound, there are two words and the preceding word governs the latter one or we can say that the first word qualifies the second word. In Determinative a compound is formed between nouns, adjectives or adverbs. This Tatpuruṣa compound is used in six types in Sanskrit— (i) Tatpuruṣa proper or the Inflection (ii) Karmadhāraya or the Appositional (iii) Nañ Tatpuruṣa or the Negative (iv) Dwigu Tatpuruṣa or the Numeral (v) Prādi/gati Tatpuruṣa or (Prepositional) Determinative (vi) Upapada Tatpuruṣa.

(i) Tatpuruṣa or the Inflectional— In this compound, the attributive element indicates any of the six oblique cases, if the compound is dissolved. Below the compound in each case is discussed—

(a) Accusative Case— A noun takes Accusative case when compounded with words like srita, atīta, patita, gata, prāpta etc.—

Kṛṣṇaśritaḥ — kṛṣṇam śritaḥ (in the refuge of lord Krishna)

dukhātītaḥ — dukham atīitaḥ (one who has overcome pain)

prāptajīvikaḥ— prāpto jīvikām (one who has obtained livelihood)

grāmagamī — grāmam gamī (going to the village)

(b) Instrumental Case— In Tatpuruṣa a noun may take Instrumental case– with another noun indicating the effect; for example—

śaṅkulākhaṇḍaḥ— śaṅkulayā khaṇḍaḥ (a piece broken with a pair of nippers)

dhānyārthaḥ— dhānyena arthaḥ (wealth begotten by means of grain)

—with verbal derivatives when the noun in Instrumental case is acting as an agent—

Nakhanirbhinnaḥ— nakhair nirbhinnaḥ (torn with nails)

haritrātaḥ — hariṇā trātaḥ (rescued by lord Vishnu)

—with words like pūrva, sadṛśa, sama etc.—

māsapūravaḥ— māsena pūrvaḥ (earlier by a month)

mātṛsadṛśaḥ— mātrā sadṛśaḥ (like his mother)

pitṛsamaḥ — pitrā samaḥ (like father)

—with another noun denoting food item; the noun with Instrumental Case also signifies some condiment or seasoning—

Dadhyodanaḥ— dadhinā odanaḥ (rice mixed with curd)

guḍadhānaḥ— guḍena dhānaḥ (rice mixed with jaggery)

Sometimes in compounds the Instrumental is not omitted, it remains there as it would be while dissolved; for example—

ojasākṛtam— ojasā kṛtam (done with energy)

añjasākṛtam— añjasā kṛtam (done with honesty)

manasāguptā— manasā guptā (a name), similarly manoguputā is also a name.

(c) Dative Case— In Tatpuruṣa, a Dative case is used

—with a noun indicating purpose; for example— yūpadāruḥ— yūpāya dāruḥ (wood for a sacrificial post)

—when words like hita, sukha, bali are compounded with—

Gohitam — gave hitam (good for a cow)

Gosukham — gave sukham (good for the cow)

bhūtabaliḥ— bhūtebhyo baliḥ (offering for other creatures)

dwijārthaḥ odanaḥ— dwijāya ayam odanaḥ (rice for Brahmana)

In certain words Dative is not dropped as in; parasmaipadam— action implied from the word for others, ātmanepadam— action implied from the word for self.

(d) Ablative Case— In Ablative Case a noun is compounded

—with words indicating fear; bhaya, bhīta, and words like apetaḥ, patitaḥ etc.—

Caurabhayam— caurād bhayam (fear from thief)

sukhāpetaḥ— sukhād apetaḥ (deprived of happiness)

swargapatitaḥ— swargād patitaḥ (fallen from heaven)

Words like stoka— little, antika— near, dūra— afar, do not drop the case in a compound; for example— stokānmuktaḥ— stokād muktaḥ (relieved from a little)

antikādāgataḥ— antikāt āgataḥ (coming from nearby place) or

dūrādāgataḥ— dūrāt āgataḥ (coming from a distance)

(e) Genitive Case— A noun in Genitive case is compounded with a noun for example—

rājapuruṣaḥ— rājñaḥ puruṣaḥ (king's man)

daśarathputraḥ— daśarathasya putraḥ (son of Dasharatha)

A noun in Genitive is not compounded with verbal derivatives which end in aka or tṛ—

Odanasya pācakaḥ can not be compounded as odanapācakaḥ, similarly ghaṭsya kartā can not be ghaṭakartā, but certain exceptions are also available in this language; for example— devasya pūjakaḥ is compounded as devapūjakaḥ (worshipper of god), in the same way rājñaḥ paricārakaḥ is compounded as rājaparicārakaḥ (attendant of the king).

Words like pūrva, carama, adhara are compounded with a noun and are placed first in a compound; for example— pūrvakāyaḥ— pūrvam kāyasya (the fore part of the body; the second noun is in singular, caramarātraḥ— caramam rātreḥ (peak of the night).

Sometimes words like pūrva, ardha denote a single object whereas the latter noun indicates the plural number, in such condition there can not be a compound—

pūrvaśchātrāṇām— the first among pupils, similarly, ardham pippalīnām (half of the berries).

When reproach is implied, the Genitive is retained in a

compound—

devānāmpriyaḥ— an idiot, otherwise it will be devapriyaḥ— dear to god, similarly caurasyakulam— gang of thieves; but in a word like brāhmaṇakulam (family of the Brahmana) the case is dropped.

In a compound, when words ending in ṛ are used with other nouns indicating blood-relation, then the case must not be dropped— hotuḥ putraḥ (son of a priest), but when such word is followed by svasṛ or pati then the omission of the case is optional—

mātṛsvasā or mātuḥ svasā (sister of the mother)

svasṛpatiḥ or svasuḥ patiḥ (husband of the sister)

(f) Locative Case— In a Tatpuruṣa, a noun takes Locative case when compounded- with words like śauṇḍa, pravīṇa, nipuṇa, kuśala etc.—

1. Akśaśauṇḍaḥ— akśeṣu śauṇḍaḥ (expert in dice)
2. vākpaṭuḥ— vāci paṭuḥ (clever in talk)
3. sabhāpaṇḍitaḥ— sabhāyām paṇḍitaḥ (scholar in assembly)

with words indicating contempt or satire, like—

1. tīrthakākaḥ— tīrthe kākaḥ (a very greedy person)
2. kūpamaṇḍūkaḥ— kūpe maṇdūkaḥ (pale of his village)

Sometimes the case is not dropped in a compound—

1. Geheśūraḥ— gehe śūraḥ (a boasting coward)
2. pātrekuśalaḥ— pātre kuśalaḥ (a good for nothing fellow or good at eating only)
3. araṇyetilakaḥ— araṇye tilakḥ (literally— wild sesamum yielding no oil— nothing turning out)
4. yudhiṣṭhiraḥ— yudhi sthiraḥ (a brave person)

The case is also not dropped when a noun is compounded with verb derivatives; for example—

1. kuśeśayaḥ— kuśe śete iti (a lotus)
2. jaleśayaḥ—jale śete iti (a fish)
3. sarasijam – sarasi jāyate iti (a lotus)
4. In the last example the case is dropped optionally, hence the compound may also be–

   Sarojam– a lotus

In some compounds the case is dropped even though the noun is compounded with verb derivatives; for example— kurucarāḥ – kuruṣu caranti (people who wander in kuru land).

(ii) Karmadhāraya or the Appositional— A karmadhāraya is a compound in which two words are appositional to each other. In this compound, generally an adjective is followed by a noun and both members take the same case. Here the base in the apposition of the two members is the similarity expressed—

1. Ghanaśyamaḥ— Ghana iva śyāmaḥ (dark like a cloud)
2. puruṣavyāghraḥ— puruṣo vyāghra iva (man like a tiger)
3. mukhacandraḥ— mukham candra iva (face like the moon)

This type of compound is known as samānādhikaraṇa tatpuruṣa. In this category, the compound indicates upamā or Simile, here the prominence is given to upamāna.

Sometimes the comparision is dissolved and the compound indicates rūpaka or Metaphor; for example— Mukhacandraḥ— mukhmeva candraḥ (face is the moon) or Mukhapadmam— mukhameva padmam (face is lotus).

At places a qualifying noun is compounded with a qualified noun; for example—

Kṛṣṇasarpaḥ— kṛṣṇaścā'sau sarpaḥ (black serpent) or nīlotpalam— nīlam ca tadutpalam (blue lotus)

In karmadhāraya, sometimes in a compound word, where two subsequent actions are indicated by first and second members, two declinable particles are used—

snātānuliptaḥ— ādau snātaḥ paścādanuliptaḥ (first bathed, then smeared)

Word kutsitaḥ changes to particle **ku** if followed by a noun indicating displeasure—

kupuruṣaḥ— kutsitaḥ puruṣaḥ (a bad man)

Kutsitaḥ changes to **kad** if it is followed by a noun having an initial vowel—

Kadaśvaḥ— kutsitaḥ aśvaḥ (a bad horse)

In some compounds, second member of the first word is dropped—

śākapārthivaḥ— śākapriyaḥ pārthivaḥ (a king who loves vegetables), in this compound the word priya is dropped; this type of compound is known as **madhyamapadalopī**.

(iii) Nañ tatpuruṣa or the Negative— When negation is indicated by a compound, it is known as nañ tatpuruṣa. In this compound, particle **na** changes to **a** or **an**. **Na** is replaced by an **a**, if it is followed by a word having an initial consonant and it is replaced by an **an** if it is followed by a word having an initial vowel; for example—

abrāhmaṇaḥ— na brāhmaṇaḥ (one who is not a Brahmin)

anaśvaḥ— na aśvaḥ (one who is not a horse)

Sometimes the particle does not take any change—

Nakulaḥ— a mongoose, nakśatram– a star

(iv) Dvigu tatpruṣa or Numeral— In a dvigu tatpuruṣa, the first member of the compound is a numeral or samkhyā, hence generally it is known as **samkhyāvācī dvigu.**

A dvigu compound indicates an aggregate and then it ends in neuter gender; such as—

1. Tribhuvanam— trayāṇām bhuvanānām samāhāraḥ (the three worlds taken together)
2. Pañcagavam— pañcānām gavām samāhāraḥ (five cows taken collectively)

A dvigu compound may also take a suffix (taddhita)—

ṣaṇmāturaḥ— ṣaṇṇām mātṛṇām apatyam (son of six mothers)

Dvigu compounds are generally found in neuter gender but they may also be used in masculine (as in above example) and feminine genders—

1. trilokī— trayāṇām lokānām samāhāraḥ (three worlds collectively)
2. pañcavaṭī— pañcānām vaṭānā samāhāraḥ (five trees collectively)

(v) a. Prādi tatpuruṣa or Prepositional Determinative— The compounds which have a preposition as the first member, are known as **prādi tatpuruṣa**; in such compounds a preposition is followed by a noun in the Nominative, Accusative etc.—

1. prācāryaḥ— pragataḥ ācāryaḥ (an eminent teacher)
2. atimālaḥ— atikrāntaḥ mālām (surpassing a garland in fragrance)
3. nirgṛhaḥ— nirgataḥ gṛhāt (got out of the house)
4. supuruṣaḥ— śobhanaḥ puruṣaḥ (a nice man)

b. Gati tatpuruṣa— In this compound, words like **ūrī, āvis, puras, śuklī** etc. are compounded with verbal indeclinables; for example—

1. ūrīkṛtya— having accepted
2. śuklīkṛtya— making white which is not
3. puraskṛtya— placing in front
4. āviṣkṛtya— having explored

These compounds may also be formed with nouns derived from roots as the second members; for example—

puraskāraḥ— showing respect

tiraskāraḥ— showing insult

(vi) upapada tatpuruṣa— In this compound, the first member is depended upon by the second member which becomes a root noun after taking **kṛt** suffix; hence it is known as **upapada tatpuruṣa—**

1. kumbhakāraḥ— kumbham karoti iti (a potter), here kumbha is upapada.
2. svarṇakāraḥ— svarṇam karoti iti (a goldsmith)
3. kambaladaḥ— kambalam dadāti iti (one who gives blanket)

There are other upapadas like uccheiḥ, nīceiḥ, tiryak etc. which take verbal indeclinables as second member; for example—

1. Uccheiḥkṛtya or kṛtvā— having made acutely or accented
2. nīceiḥkṛtya— having made a low tone
3. tiryakkṛtya— having laid aside

General Rules followed in Tatpuruṣa—

*Word **rātri** used in a compound, takes **a** as a final vowel if it follows a numeral or an indeclinable; for example—

1. sarvarātraḥ— sarvā ratriḥ (whole night)
2. dvirātram— dvayoḥ ratryoḥ samāhāraḥ (total two nights)

This rule also follows when **rātri** word is preceded by word **ahan—**

ahorātraḥ— ahaśca rātriśca (day and night)

*The gender of a collective **dvigu** is neutral; if such

compound ends in **a,** than it takes feminine gender. The termination may be **ī** for both compounds ending in **a** or **ā**; for example—

1. trilokī— trayāṇām lokānām samāhāraḥ (three worlds collectively)
2. pañcakhaṭvī— pañcānām khaṭvānām samāhāraḥ (five cots together)

*The **na** of word **Brāhmaṇa** in a compound is not seen—

mahābrahma— mahānścā'sau brāhmaṇaḥ (a great Brahmana)

kubrahma— kutsitaḥ brāhmaṇaḥ (a degraded Brahmana)

2. Dvandva or Copulative Compound— In this compound two or more nouns are joined together, when dissolved they are connected by a copulative particle **ca**; for example—

1. mātāpitarau— mātā ca pitā ca (parents)
2. bharatalakśmaṇaśtrughnāḥ — bharataśca lakśmaṇaśca śatrughnaśca (names of the sons of king Dasharath)

This dvandva is found in three types— itaretara dvandva, samāhāra dvandva and ekaśeṣa dvandva. Some scholars do not consider ekaśeṣa in the dvandva category, since it does not consist of more than one noun (subanta).

a. Itaretara dvandva— In this dvandva , all the members are treated separately, they all have equal importance and they are capable of denoting separate meaning. The nouns can be in dual or plural number, the gender of the compound is determined by the gender of the final noun; for example—

1. kukkuṭamayūryau— kukkuṭaśca mayūrī ca (a cock and a peahen), in this word the final noun is in feminine gender, hence the compound ends in feminine gender;

whereas in mayūrīkukkuṭau— mayūrī ca kukkuṭaśca (a peahen and a cock) the final noun is in masculine gender, therefore it ends in masculine gender.

2. dhavakhadirau— dhavaśca khadiraśca (names of trees), here both nouns take masculine gender.

We find some instances where this rule of final gender is not strictly followed, as in the following example— ahorātraḥ— ahaśca rātriśca (day and night), here in this word even though the final member is in feminine gender, the compound ends in masculine gender.

b. Samāhāra dvandva— Samāhāra means 'aggregate or collective'. In such compound, all the members denote the aggregate of the things and they indicate a complex idea. This compound may have more than two members, but the final member will take singular number in neuter gender; for example—

1. āhāranidrābhayam— āhāraśca nidrā ca bhayaśca (food, sleep and fear together) literally, but the compound means all the abovementioned things which symbolise animal life.

2. pāṇipādam— pāṇī ca pādau ca (hands and feet together; parts of the body)

*When a compound denotes limbs or body-parts, musical players, segments of army, rivers, countries etc., it always ends in neutral gender singular number; for example—

1. rathikāśvāroham— rathikāśca aśvārohāśca (chariot-warriors and horsemen)
2. mārdaṅgikapāṇavikam— mārdaṅgikaśca pāṇavikaśca (a drummer and a player of a cymbal)
3. gaṅgāśoṇam— gaṅgā ca śoṇaśca (the Ganges and Son rivers), but in
4. gaṅgāyamune— gaṅgā ca yamunā ca (The Ganges and The Yamuna) both nouns are of the same genders;

therefore the compound is taking feminine gender in dual number in the final.

*Names of fruits, herbs, birds-animals etc., if constituted in plural number, take singular number in neuter gender in the final—

1. badarāmalakam— badarāṇi ca āmalakāni ca (a collection of berries and mangoes)
2. gavāśvam— gāvaśca aśvāśca (herd of cows and horses)

*if the members of this compound are in singular number, then the gender will follow the final member in dual number—

1. badarāmalake— badaram ca āmalakam ca (a berry and an emblic)
2. rathikāśvārohau— rathikaśca aśvārohaśca (a chariot-warrior and a horseman)

*If words indicating blood-relation end with ṛ, then this ṛ changes to ā—

1. mātāpitarau— mātā ca pitā ca (parents)
2. pitāputrau— pitā ca putraśca (father and son)

*When names of popular deities known to be associated with each other, are in a compound, then the last vowel of the preceding noun takes an ā—

1. mitrāvaruṇau— mitraśca varuṇaśca (the sun and rain-god)
2. sūryācandramasau— sūryaśca candramasaśca (the sun and the moon)

*There are certain exceptions also in practice in this regard—

1. agnivāyū— agniśca vāyuśca (fire and wind) or
2. vāyvāgnī— vāyuśca agniśca (wind and fire)

*other irregular examples can also be seen in this

compound—

1. dyāvāpṛthivyau— dyauśca pṛthivī ca (heaven and earth)
2. jāyāpatī— jāyā ca patiśca (wife and husband)
3. strīpumānsau— strī ca pumānśca (woman and man)
4. putrapautram— putrāśca pautrāśca (sons and grandsons)

In the abovementioned examples we come across a practice that in compounds which consist of male and female members, a female noun precedes a male noun. A noun having less phonemes precedes the other noun, a noun reflecting more respect, precedes the other noun in a compound.

c. **Ekaśeṣa dvandva**— In this compound only one word is retained which indicates the required number of all members used; for example—

1. pitarau— mātā ca pitā ca (parents)

   Śvaśurau— śvaśrūśca śvaśuraśca (parents-in-law)

*In the compound when there are nouns indicating same form, only one noun is retained with the required number—

rāmaśca rāmaśca rāmaśca— rāmāḥ (persons of name Rama)

The abovesaid practice is seen with different forms also—

Vakradaṇḍau— vakradaṇḍaśca kuṭiladaṇḍaśca (curved and crooked bamboos) or

Kuṭiladaṇḍau— kuṭiladaṇḍaśca vakradaṇḍaśca (crooked and curved bamboos)

In compounds consisting male and female nouns, male noun is retained—

Haṁsau— haṁsī ca haṁsaśca (swans)

brāhmaṇau— brāhmaṇī ca brāhmaṇaśca (man and woman of Brahmana caste)

3. Bahuvrīhi or Attributive Compound— A Bahuvrīhi compound is a compound in which two or more nouns in apposition to each other, are the constituents; in this the attributive member is placed first and it denotes or qualifies something which is not denoted by the members. It also attributes what is expressed by the other noun, sometimes the substantive is not in apposition with the other members of the compound; for example—

1. nīlakaṇṭhaḥ— nīlam kaṇṭham yasya saḥ (lord Shiva)
2. pītāmbaraḥ— pītam ambaram yasya saḥ (lord Vishnu)
3. dattacittaḥ— dattam cittam yena saḥ (a pupil)

Compounds are of two types— (i) samānādhikaraṇa bahuvrīhi (ii) vyadhikaraṇa bahuvrīhi.

(i) Samānādhikaraṇa Bahuvrīhi— A samānādhikaraṇa bahuvrīhi consists of the members which are in apposition with each other and they take the same case when they are dissolved. The members of the compound may take all the six cases of word **yat;** for example—

1. ārūḍhvānaraḥ— ārūḍhaḥ vānaraḥ yam saḥ (tree with monkey) accus. Case
2. jitendriyaḥ— jitāni indriyāṇi yena saḥ (a disciplined man) instr. case
3. dattadhanaḥ— dattam dhanam yasmei saḥ (a brahmana) Dat. case
4. nirdhanaḥ— nirgatam dhanam yasmāt saḥ (a poor man) Abl. Case
5. lambakarṇaḥ— lambau karṇau yasya saḥ (a donkey) Gen. case

vīrapuruṣaḥ— vīrāḥ puruṣāḥ yasmin saḥ (a village having brave persons) Loc. case

(ii) Vyadhikaraṇa comound— In vyadhikaraṇa

compound, the members are not in apposition with each other and they take different cases when dissolved, unlike samānādhikaraṇa,—

1. Candraśekharaḥ— candraḥ śekhare yasya saḥ (lord Shiva)
2. cakrapāṇiḥ— cakram pāṇau yasya saḥ (lord Vishnu)
3. In vyadhikaraṇa compound first member takes Nominative case and second member takes Genitive or Locative case, when the compound is dissolved.

Bahuvrīhi, further can be divided into two parts— tadguṇasaṁvijñāna and atadguṇasaṁvijñāna bahuvrīhi.

Tadguṇasaṁvijñāna bahuvrīhi is the one in which the sense of the attributive member is also denoted; for example—

pītāmbaram harim preṣaya (send Hari who is in yellow clothes), it indicates Hari who has yellow attire and in **atadguṇasaṁvijñāna**, the sense of the attributive member is not denoted; for example—

śvetagum gopam āhvaya (call that herdsman who has white cow), here the herdsman is referred not the white cow.

*Bahuvrīhi compounds with negative particles **a** or **an** are used with substantives, sometimes verb-derivatives indicate the meaning when dissolved—

1. Aputraḥ— avidyamānaḥ putraḥ yasya saḥ (a father without a son)
2. Praparṇaḥ— prapatitāni parṇāni yasya saḥ (a tree with its leaves dropped)

*Sometimes prepositions are also used in such compounds—

1. utkandharaḥ— udgatā kandharā yasya saḥ (having the neck erect)

2. vijīvitaḥ— vigatam jīvitam yasya saḥ (a dead person)

*The particle **saha** used with a noun is also found in this compound; the noun takes Instrumental case and the particle optionally changes to **sa**—

Sahaputraḥ or saputraḥ— putreṇa saha (with son)

Particle **saha** does not take any change if a blessing is indicated—

Svasti rājñe sahaputrāya (may the king be blessed with son), here **saha** remains unchanged.

General Rules followed in Bahuvrīhi— *The compound consisting of feminine words ends in **a,** if pramāṇī word is used as a second member—

strīpramāṇaḥ— strī pramāṇī yasya asau (one whose authority is a woman)

When **pramāṇī** word is not used and the compound indicates compliment; it ends in **a—** kalyāṇī pañcamā rātrayaḥ— kalyāṇī pañcamī yāsām rātrīṇām tāḥ (nights whose complement is the auspicious fifth night)

*In the end of the compound, word **jāyā** changes to **jāni—**

yuvajāniḥ— yuvatī jāyā yasya saḥ (one whose wife is young) or

bhūjāniḥ— bhūḥ jāyā yasya saḥ (one whose wife is earth— a king)

- Word **nāsikā** changes to **nasa** if it is preceded by a preposition—

Unnasaḥ— udgatā nāsikā yasya saḥ (having a prominent nose), similarly

Praṇasaḥ— pragatā nāsikā yasya saḥ (one having a nice nose)

- Word **hṛdaya** changes to **hṛd**, if it is preceded by

prepositions like **su** or **dus**—

Suhṛd— śobhanam hṛdayam yasya saḥ (a person having a noble heart) or

Durhṛd— duṣṭam hṛdayam yasya saḥ (a wicked man)

- When two identical words are used to form a compound in the Locative or the Instrumental case, indicating fight, the last vowel of the words is lengthened—
- keśākeśī— keśeṣu keśeṣu gṛhītvā idam yuddham pravṛttam (a fight seizing each other's hair), similarly
- daṇḍādaṇḍī— daṇḍiśca daṇḍiśca prahṛtya idam yuddham pravṛttam (battle by striking sticks)

Some Irregularities found in Bahuvrīhi— There are some irregularities also in this compound which we can find at times; such as—

1. suprātaḥ— śobhanam prātaḥ asya (one having an auspicious morning)
2. sudivaḥ— śobhanam divā asya (one having spent a nice day)

Words like **uras, sarpiṣ** are affixed with **ka** in this compound—

1. vyūḍhoraskaḥ— vyūdham uraḥ yasya saḥ (having a broad chest)
2. priyasarpiṣkaḥ— priyam sarpiḥ yasya saḥ (a person fond of ghee)

In certain compounds the last noun ends in masculine gender—

1. rūpavadbhāryaḥ— rūpavatī bhāryā yasya saḥ (a person who has a beautiful wife)
2. sukeśībhāryaḥ— sukeśābhāryā yasya saḥ (a person whose wife has nice hair)

Karmadhāraya and Bahuvrīhi— Karmadhāraya and

Bahuvrīhi compounds may look same, but the difference lies in the technicality of their dissolution. In Karmadhāraya compound only one member is in apposition with the substantive to which it qualifies, where as in Bahuvrīhi the whole compound acts as a qualifier and the qualified is something else; for example word **gambhīranādaḥ** when dissolved as **gambhīraścā'sau nādaḥ** (a deep sound) gives a complete meaning; hence it is a karmadhāraya. The same word becomes bahuvrīhi if it is dissolved like '**gambhīraḥ nādaḥ yasya saḥ** (a person who has a deep voice), similarly, word **mahābāhuḥ** when dissolved like **mahān bāhuḥ** (a great arm) is karmadhāraya, but when dissolved as **mahān bāhū yasya saḥ** (a person who has great arms—king), it denotes bahuvrīhi.

In a vedic mantra '**indraśatrurvardhasva**' if the word **indraśatruḥ** is interpreted as tatpuruṣa then the compound will be dissolved like **indrasya śatruḥ** (vṛttra— a demon), but if it is treated as bahuvrīhi compound then it is dissolved like **indraḥ yaḥ vṛttrasya śatruḥ.**

In case of a comparision involved, the compound may be treated as bahuvrīhi otherwise it will be tatpuruṣa such as—**candrakāntiḥ**— **candrasya kāntiḥ** (moonlight) **tatpuruṣa** and in **candrasyeva kāntiryasya saḥ** (a person whose glow is like moonlight) it is bahuvrīhi.

4. Avyayībhāva or Adverbial Compound— An Avyayībhāva compound is a compound in which an indeclinable like a preposition or an adverb is joined with another member which is a noun. The compound thus formed ends in neutral gender singular number; for example—

1. upagaṅgam— gaṅgāyāḥ samīpam (near the Ganga)
2. anugaṅgam— gaṅgāyāḥ samipam (alongside the Ganga)
3. adhyātmam— ātmani iti (in the soul)
4. pratyaham— ahani ahani iti (everyday)

5. yathāśakti— śaktimanatikramya (according to one's ability)

In Avyayībhāva—

*the final long vowel is sometimes shortened as in upagaṅgam.

*The ending phoneme **n** is dropped in masculine and feminine nouns and optionally in neuter nouns; for example—

1. uparājam— rājñaḥ samīpam (near the king), here **n** of rājan is dropped in the compound.
2. upasīmam— sīmnaḥ samīpe (near the boundary)

*the **a** is optionally substituted with final vowel—

1. upanadam/upanadī (near the river)
2. upagiram/upagiri (near the mountain)

* **a** is added to the last consonant of the noun like śarad, diś, manas etc. in the compound—

Upaśaradam (near the autumn), upadiśam (between two regions), pratyakśam (in front).

*In Avyayībhāva the indeclinables are used in various cases to present different interpretations—

1. upakṛṣṇam— kṛṣṇasya samīpam (near Krishna)
2. nirmakśikam— makśikāṇām abhāvaḥ (having no flies— no disturbance)
3. adhihari— harāviti (in Hari)

*With prepositions like apa, pari, bahiḥ, the noun in Ablative case is compounded optionally—

1. Apaviṣṇu/apaviṣṇoḥ (away from Vishnu)
2. bahirvanam/bahirvanāt (out of the forest)

*With preposition **ā** indicating limit (inclusive or exclusive) the noun in Ablative case is compounded optionally—

1. āmuktiḥ/āmukteḥ (until final liberation)
2. ābālam/ābālebhyaḥ (upto the children)

When relations by blood or by lineage are indicated, the numeral with a noun may be optionally compounded—

trimunivyākaraṇam/vyākaraṇasya trimuni (the three sages of Sanskrit Grammar)

Karmadhāraya, Bahuvrīhi and Avyayībhāva—

Karmadhāraya— In Karmadharaya, the indeclinable word like **ku, pra** etc. are compounded with words which they qualify; for example—

Kupuruṣaḥ— a sinful man Or supuruṣaḥ— a gentle man

Words like **puraḥ** (in front) are also compounded with verbs—

Puraskṛtya— having put in front

Puraskaroti— puts in front

Word **astam** compounded with verb is also used in karmadhāraya—

astaṁgatāni dhanāni— riches that have vanished

In such words, the indeclinable is the qualifier of the subsequent word and when joined with noun, it takes the number and gender of the subsequent noun.

Bahuvrīhi—

In Bahuvrīhi too, the indeclinables, such as **asti** are compounded with nouns—

astikśīrābrāhmaṇī— a Brahmana woman who is having milk

Indeclinable **upa** is compounded with numerals—

upadaśāḥ— those who are about ten; may be nine or eleven

Preposition like **ut** is also compounded with words like **nāsikā** , **gandhi** etc.—

1. Unnasaḥ—one having a prominent nose
2. udgandhiḥ—one whose fragrance is around

With preposition **ā**

1. ājārasa— reaching old age
2. āpathi— being in the way

With negative particle

1. aputraḥ—a person who does not have a son
2. nirghṛṇaḥ—merciless cruel

Avyayībhāva— The avyayībhāva compound is constructed invariably with an adverb, a preposition or a particle as a first member and a noun which is the subsequent member. The compound may indicate all cases in the final noun (when dissolved) but it will end in neuter gender singular number in the Nominative case.

Compounds like atimātra (excessive) which are treated as adjectival compounds, are considered as Bahuvrīhi; whereas compounds like atimātram (excessively) which are known as adverbial compounds, fall in the category of Avyayībhāva compounds.

Compounds in Indo-European Languages—

The traces of Sanskrit compounds like **karmadhāraya** can be found in Greek and Latin languages; for example— Greek word ἰατρòμαντις means 'physian seer'.

Many words in **tatpuruṣa** compound can also be seen in IE languages—

1. Muscerda (Latin)— mouse-dung
2. Piudangardi (Gothik)— king's house
3. Vodotoku (Old Slavonik)— water-house

These compounds were used without the inflection for

any gender, number or case.

Compounds with verbal component as second member are also in use in IE languages—

Artifex (Latin)— something artistic

Compounds with thematic suffix are also available in IE languages—

Hasidava (Avestan)— betraying a friend

This trend of compound words is found even in Russian language—

Vodons— water-carrier

Bahuvrīhi compound is also found in use in IE languages—

(Greek) λευkωλευος— white-armed

(Latin) Magnanimou— great-souled

(Latin) capricornus— having goat's horns

(Gothik) hrainya-hairts – pure-hearted

(Old Slavonic) crǐnovlasǔ — black haired

Certain type of compounds, which are available only in Vedic literature, can also be traced in Indo-European languages—

(Avestan) vanat pəsǎna— winning battles

(Greek) ελkεόίπεπλος — dragging robes

The use of dvandva compound can be seen in Avestan; such as—

Pasu vira— beast and man

āpa urvaire— water and crops

Though nouns in feminine gender in the dvandva compounds were not used in the early Vedic texts, but they were known in Avestan language.

VI.2

Compound in Manipuri

Manipuri language has a tradition of compounding two or more linguistic elements, those could be verb and noun, verb and verb or noun and noun and so on. Therefore, there are types of compounds like noun compound, adjective compound verb compound etc. We can divide these compounds in two categories— semantically classified compounds and form- based compounds.

1. **Semantically classified compounds—**
   There are two types of compounds in this category—
   (a) Endocentric and Exocentric,
   (b) Co-ordinate Compounds

(a) Endocentric Compounds—

An Endocentric compound consists of a 'head' and its modifiers, the 'head' contains the basic meaning of a compound and the 'modifiers' restrict the meaning. In this compound the referent is the same as the referent of one of its constituent parts; for example—the noun 'Blackboard' is Endocentric, in this it refers to a type of a board. This compound is further subdivided into two types; Right-Headed and Left-Headed as based on the attribution.

Right-Headed Compound—

In the Right-Headed compound, both members generally happen to be nouns. The two nouns are related with each other by possessive suffix gi/ki or there may be one of the several bases that do not actually have a role in the compound. The examples are as given below—

Compounds indicating possessive relations—

(i) mayrī — may gi marī

flame — fire of string

(ii) unā — u gi manā
leaf — tree of leaf

(iii) mitpān — mit gi mapān
eyelid — eye of outer part

(iv) khuniṅ — khud gi maniṅ
elbow — arm of back

Compounds indicating possessive in the meaning of direction—

(i)	yumthak	—	yum	gi	mathak
	terrace	—	house	of	top
(ii)	khoṅgsā	—	khoṅ	gi	masā
	toe	—	foot	of	part

In Manipuri, generally nominal bound roots (nouns) are affixed with a third person pronominal marker '**ma**' in the structure, this prefix is omitted in a compound.

Compounds having verbs relating nouns—

(i)	mirān	—	mi na	sāba	lān
	cobweb	—	spider erg.	make	trap
(ii)	laumi	—	lau	uba	mi
	Farmer	—	field	cultivate	person
(iii)	mayrik	—	may	dagi	marik
	spark	—	fire	from	pieces

From these abovementioned examples it is clear that the second member is a verb- related noun. There are more examples of compounds, indicating different constructions—

(i)	thumhī	— thum	yāoba	mahī	
	saline water	— salt	containing	water	
(ii)	ciṅmi	— ciṅ	da	layba	mi
	tribal	— hill	loc.	living	people
(iii)	tammi	— tam	da	layba	mi
	People of the valley	— valley	loc.	living	people

There are other types of compounds which consist of three words—noun + verb + noun; we can interpret that they consist of two free or bound roots joined with a dynamic root. In such compounds the verb relates the two nouns—

(i)	mithunsān	— mi	thunnaba	sān	
	a shelter for people	— people	arrive	house	
(ii)	khutsūman	— khud	na	sūbagi	maman
	wages	— hand	instr.	work of	price

Some compounds consist of noun and verb—

(i)	lāyniṅ	— lāy	bu	niṅgba
	prayer	— god	accus.	pray
(ii)	lamsī	— lam	da	sībā
	death outside	— road	loc.	die

Some compounds have action-related root as first member and word like **'mapham** or **pham'** as the second member and this '**pham**' (place) word becomes a part of the compound—

(i)	lotpham	— lotnaba	mapham
	hiding place	— hiding	place
(ii)	thoṅpham	— thoṅgnaba	mapham
	kitchen	— cooking	place
(iii)	yonpham	— yonnaba	mapham
	shop	— selling	place

There are other examples also—

(i)	lāypham	— lāy	gi	mapham
	temple	— god	ben.	place
(ii)	laupham	— lau	gi	mapham
	paddy field	— paddy	ben.	place
(iii)	maypham	— may	haunaba	mapham
	fire place	— fire	start	place

Left-Headed Compound—

In the Left-Headed compound the second member is

the head; that is a noun and the first member is generally an attributive—

(i) potlum — arumba pot
load — heavy thing

(ii) thāsī — asība thā
new moon — dead moon

(iii) wāsāṅ — asāṅgba wā
whole bamboo — tall bamboo

(iv) phijet — setnaba phi
dress — wear cloth

(v) caysū — sūnaba cay
walking stick — hitting ground stick

Last two compounds indicate the relationship in the constituent parts. Some Left-Headed compounds can be seen having both members joined with gi/ki marker, without the change in their position—

(i) laypāl	—	laybāk	gi	pāl
wall of mud	—	mud	gen.	fence
(ii) thāmay	—	thā	gi	mamay
end of the month	—	month	gen.	tail

(b) Exocentric Compound—

An Exocentric compound is a compound whose referent is not the same as are the referents of any of its constituent parts. Such compounds represent a head which is not expressed by any of its constituent parts. In Manipuri, these compounds consist of a noun and a bound root or both bound roots. Since both the elements can not be taken as head, words like **'pot'** (thing) or **'mi'** (man) are added to indicate it. These compounds are found in two types— (i) Compound indicating purpose and (ii) Compound indicating result.

Compound indicating Purpose—

There are certain words which express purpose between

two elements of the compound—

(i) monkhum — mon da khumnaba pot
pillow cover — pillow loc. cover thing

(ii) khoṅji — khoṅ da sinaba pot
anklet — foot loc. wear thing

(iii) kāṅgkhan — kāṅ khannaba pot
mosquito net — mosquito prevent thing

Compound indicating Result—

Certain compound words indicate result—

(i)	phayjup	—	phay	supnaba	phī
	quilt	—	thigh	cover	cloth

Some compounds convey **'mī'** (man) or **'nupī'** (woman), the examples are given below—

(i) puṅyāyba — puṅ yāyba (mī)
drummer — drum beat to (man)

(ii) ūsūba — ū sūba (mī)
carpenter — wood work (man)

(iii) phiyonbī — phi yonba (nupī)
cloth merchant woman — cloth sell to (woman)

(iv) kwāyonbī — kwā yonba (nupī)
betal selling woman — betal sell (woman)

It may also convey a particular thing—

(i) ukābī — u da kāba ṅgā
a kind of fish — tree loc. climb fish

(ii)	mayrānbī	—	may	da	lānba	tin
	moth	—	fire	loc.	die	insect

It may also convey **'mapham'** (place) as a referent—

(i) potyonpham — pot yonbā mapham
market/shop — thing sell place

(ii) torbān — toren gi mapān
river bank — river gen. bank

(c) Co-ordinate Compound—

In a Co-ordinate compound both members act as heads, generally they are nouns joined together with suffix **ga/ka, amasuṅ, amadī** etc.—

(i) sāsen — sā amadi sen
cattle — animal and cow

(ii) macāmasu — macā ga masu ga
off spring — son and grandchild

(iii) khoṅkhud — khoṅ ga khud ga
limbs — feet and hands

In this type of compound, neither of the elements is attribute, they both complement each other.

2. Form-Based Compounds—

In Manipuri grammar, compounds are categorized on the basis of forms also, the constituent elements may be noun + noun, noun + verb, or noun + verb + noun but the resultant compound generally ends up as a Noun—

Compound Elements

	Compound		Element		Element
	Noun	—	Noun	+	Noun
(i)	mirān	—	mi	+	lān
	cobweb	—	Spider	+	trap
(ii)	ciṅmi	—	ciṅg	+	mi
	tribal	—	Hill	+	people
(iii)	mamāmacā	—	mamā	+	macā
	mother and child	—	Mother	+	child
	Nominal	—	Noun	+	Verb
(i)	puṅyāyba	—	puṅ	+	yāyba
	drummer	—	drum	+	beat
(ii)	nuṅsūba	—	nuṅ	+	sūba
	mason	—	stone	+	work
	Noun	—	Noun	+	Adjective
(ii)	yumthak	—	yum	+	mathak

	roof	—	house	+	top
(iii)	mitpān	—	mit	+	pān
	eyelid	—	eye	+	outside
(iv)	ciṅjāo	—	ciṅ	+	cāoba
	mountain	—	hill	+	large
	Noun	—	Adjective	+	Noun
(i)	potlum	—	arumba	+	pot
	load	—	heavy	+	object
(ii)	thāsi	—	asība	+	thā
	new moon	—	dead	+	moon

Sometimes, adjectives having noun + verb as elements form the compound—

Adjective	—	Noun	+	Verb
lamkoy (wārī)	—	lam	+	koy
travelogue	—	place	+	tour

Compounds with three elements—

	Noun	—	Noun	+	Verb	+	Noun
(i)	hayyonpham	—	hay	+	yonba	+	mapham
	fruit stall	—	fruit	+	sell	+	place
(ii)	mithunsān	—	mi	+	thun	+	sān
	shelter-house	—	men	+	arrive	+	house

Compounds having Affixes—

In Manipuri some compounds are formed by adding prefixes, this formation is known as Affixo-Compounding—

(i)	atuman	—	a	+	tu man (maman)
	stitching charges	—	pref.	+	stitch charges
(ii)	atākman	—	a	+	tāk man (maman)
	tution fee	—	pref.	+	tution charges

Some new compounds are rapidly finding place in Manipuri language, these compounds are recognized as coined words by linguists. These words seem to be formed as need-based, for example—

(i)	yāwonloy	—	yāwon	+	loy
	revọlutionary	—	change	+	person
(ii)	wākhanlon	—	wākhan	+	lon
	philosophy	—	thought	+	language
(iii)	mahaykol	—	mahay	+	kol
	school	—	study	+	place

Compounds by Doubling Words—

There is a tendency among Manipuri people to use compounds by doubling words, these words are known as **'wāhei-leitān'** which itself is the result of doubling of words. Both words indicate the same meaning; the second word is used to put an emphasis to it or to give it a plural impression—

(i) wāri – watāi — stories
(ii) phi - ron — clothes
(iii) phamuṅ – phānuṅ — bedding

Conclusion

Sanskrit has a rich tradition of using compound words. One can see in Vedic literature that generally two stems are compounded in a word. It was only in the later period that poets started concentrating on the finesse of the language. They used more elaborate style and in that stepped in the more complex and difficult combination of elements. Poets like Bāṇa, Bhāravi, Kālidāsa have earned reputation of using beautiful, very meaningful and very complex compound words in their works.

Compound is an important part of speech. The richness of any language can be valued by the variety and range of grammatical aspects, form and construction, style and writing etc. Compound is an integral element in Manipuri language also. There, a lot of variation is found, for example— a compound can be formed between a verb and a noun, a verb and a verb or a noun and an adjective etc. There may be compounds consisting of more than two roots also.

Similarities—

The style of compound words in Manipuri language is generally found quite similar to that of Sanskrit. The Right-Headed Compounds in the Endocentric category have the same type of formations as we find in Tatpuruṣa in Sanskrit. Tatpuruṣa allows Accusative to Locative case to be the tool in compounding words. In Manipuri, in the Endocentric compound Genitive case-suffix is seen in use very often, besides this, Instrumental and Locative suffix is also used. There are many compound words which are having Accusative case-suffix also; for example—

lāyniṅ	—	Lāy	bu	niṅba
prayer	—	God	accu.	pray

*In Sanskrit in Tatpuruṣa, 'Madhyamapadalopīsamāsa' is formed as in **śākapārthivaḥ**, when dissolved it is **śākapriyaḥ pārhtivaḥ**, similarly, in Manipuri, Right-Headed compounds have a trend of this type of construction; for example—

Thummī	—	thum	yāobā	mahī
Saline water	—	salt	containing	liquid

*The Sanskrit Karmadhāraya and Manipuri Left-Headed compounds have a lot in common. In Karmadhāraya, the adjective which is a qualifier, is compounded with a noun which is the head. In Left-Headed compound also the first member is an adjective which attributes the second member, the only difference is that the attribute and head interchange their positions; for example—

Karmadhāraya—

(i)	nīlotpalam	—	nīlam	ca	tadudpalam
	Blue lotus	—	blue	and	that lotus
(ii)	kṛṣṇasarpaḥ	—	kṛṣṇaścā̦'sau		sarpaḥ
	black serpant	—	black	and	that serpant

Left-Headed compound—

(i) Potlum — arumbā pot
Load — heavy object

(ii) thāsī — asībā thā
new moon — dead moon

*Exocentric compound, in Manipuri language has two members but the referent of the compound indicates other than the referent of the members. In Bahuvrīhi too, in Sanskrit, two nouns are placed in apposition to each other but neither of the members is qualified by the compound. It qualifies something else which is not related to the constituting members, the examples are—

Exocentric Compound—

(i) monkhum — mon dā khumnaba pot
pillow case — pillow loc. cover thing

(ii) kāṅkhan — kāṅ khannaba pot
mosquito net — mosquito prevent thing

Bahuvrīhi —

(i) pītāmbaraḥ — pītam ambaram yasya saḥ
Vishnu — yellow dress whose he

(ii) nīlakaṇṭhaḥ — nīlam kaṇṭham yasya saḥ
Shiva — blue throat whose he

*Manipuri Co-ordinate compound is constituted of two words— both words are Heads and they co-ordinate with each other as it is indicated by the name itself. This compound acts in the same manner as Dvandva in Sanskrit. In Dvandva two or more nouns are joined with particle '**ca**' and in Manipuri Co-ordinate the words are joined with '**ga/ka**, **amasuṅ**' etc.

Co-ordinate Compound—

(i) mamāmacā — mamā ga macā ga
mother-child — mother ass. child ass.

(ii) khoṅkhud	—	khoṅ	ga	khud	ga
limbs	—	foot	ass.	hand	ass.

Dvandva —

(i) Śabdārthau	—	sábdaśca	arthaśca
word-meaning	—	word and	meaning

*In Manipuri language, compounds are also formed by doubling words; for example—

(i) wārī-watāi — stories

(ii) phamuṅ-phānuṅ — bedding

In Sanskrit too, there is a provision of such formations by doubling the indeclinables—

(i) Śaneiḥ-śaneiḥ — slowly-slowly

(ii) yathā-tathā — by all means or

yathā-yathā — so much so that

Dissimilarities—

In Manipuri:

*Form-based compound consisting Noun + Verb is a different kind of form which we do not find in Sanskrit—

(i) Nuṅsūba	—	nuṅ + sūba
Mason	—	stone + work to
(ii) puṅyāyba	—	puṅ + yāyaba
drummer	—	drum + beat to

*Sometimes the compound consists of noun + verb + noun, but in Sanskrit this type of combination is not found. There we see only noun + noun + noun—

(i) phīyonpham	—	phī	yonba	mapham
cloth-shop	—	cloth	sell	place
(ii) mīthuṅsān	—	mī	thuṅ	sān
shelter-house	—	men	arrive	house

Sanskrit—

rāmalakśmaṇabharatāḥ	—	rāmaśca lakśmaṇaśca bharataśca

(Names of three brothers compounded)

* In certain words **'a'** is affixed to the first member of the compound—

atuman	—	a	tu	man (maman)
stitching charges	—	prefix	stitch	charges

*In modern times, the use of coined words is becoming a favorite form, this type of compound expresses a specific meaning—

(i)	wākhanlon	—	wā	khanlon
	philosophy	—	thought	language
(ii)	mahāykol	—	mahāy	kol
	school or college	—	study	place

*In Left-headed Compounds, the head and attribute change their positions—

(i)	potlum	—	arumba	pot
	load	—	heavy	thing
(ii)	wāsāṅ	—	asāṅba	wā
	wholebamboo	—	tall	bamboo

In Karmadhāray, in Sanskrit the head and the qualifier do not interchange their places—

raktakamalaḥ	—	raktaśca'sau	kamalaśca
Red lotus	—	red and	this lotus

In Sanskrit:

*The application of Tatpuruṣa is varied, Nañ Tatpuruṣa Compound is used to indicate negation and the particle is **'a or an'**—

(i) anaśvaḥ — na aśvaḥ
not horse — not horse

(ii) aśvetaḥ — na śvetaḥ
not white — not white

*Words are compounded with numerals—

(i) pañcarātram — pañcānām rātrīṇām samāhāraḥ
five nights — total of five nights

(ii) trilokī — trayāṇām lokānām samāhāraḥ
three worlds — total of three worlds

*Use of Prepositional Tatpuruṣa can be seen in Sanskrit aplenty—

(i) prācāryaḥ — pragataḥ ācāryaḥ
an eminent teacher

(ii) nirgṛhaḥ — nirgataḥ gṛhāt
got out of the house

*Upapada Tatpuruṣa is commonly used in Sanskrit—

(i) kumbhakārah — kumbham karoti iti
potter — one who makes pitcher

(ii) kambaladaḥ — kambalam dadāti iti
blanket provider — one who gives blanket

*In Dvandva, sometimes one word is retained out of the two—

(i) pitarau — mātā ca pitā ca
parents — mother and father

(ii) śvaśurau — śvasrūśca śvaśuraśca
parents- in-law — mother-in-law and father-in-law

*In Bahuvrīhi, words are compounded with negative particles also—

(i) aputraḥ — avidyamānaḥ putraḥ yasya saḥ
without a son — one who does not have a son

(ii) praparṇaḥ — prapatitāni parṇāni yasmāt saḥ
tree without leaves — whose leaves have fallen

Compounds are used with **'saha'** particle—

Saputraḥ or sahaputraḥ — With a son

*The use of Avyayībhāva is a unique application in Sanskrit language which we do not find in Manipuri language. This compound consists of an indeclinable and a noun—

(i) abhihari — harau
in hari (visnu)

(ii) pratyaham — ahaḥ ahaḥ prati
daily.

VII.1

Pronoun in Sanskrit

A Pronoun, in grammar and linguistics, is termed as a substitute used for noun or noun-phrase. The Latin word for it is 'Pronomen'. Generally noun remains the antecedent for it, but a pronoun can be used even without an antecedent. A new term for a pronoun, referring to its antecedent is known as 'Anaphora'; an anphor also refers to objects that have already been discussed in the same text, for example— Shyama brought a book for Manu, she gave it to her. Here in the second clause, in the sentence 'she' 'it' and 'her' are anaphors which take reference from their antecedents.

In Sanskrit 35 words have been termed as Pronouns which are as follows; sarva, viśva, ubha, ubhaya, ḍatara, ḍatama, anya, anyatara, itara, tvat, tva, nema, sama, sima, pūrva, para, avara,dakśiṇa, uttara, apara, adhara, sva, antara, tyad, tad, yad, etad, idam, adas, eka, dvi, yuṣmad, asmad, bhavat and kim. These words are classified into different types of pronouns, such as— 1. Personal Pronoun 2. Demonstrative Pronoun 3. Relative Pronoun 4. Interrogative Pronoun 5. Indefinite Pronoun 6. Reflexive Pronoun 7. Correlative Pronoun 8. Reciprocal Pronoun and 9. Possessive Pronoun

1. Personal Pronoun— Asmad (indicating 1st person), yuṣmad (indicating 2nd person) and bhavad (2nd person respectfully), are used as Personal Pronoun. Word tvam is used for junior or equal and even superiors in 2nd person. Word bhavān or bhavatī indicates respect to 2nd person. This pronoun may be used in plural number for a person, to express great respect; for example— bhavantaḥ eva sutarām lokavṛttāntaniṣṇātāḥ. (abhijñanaśakuntalam 5 canto) The meaning is 'you are clever in worldly affairs'. These pronouns sometimes, are not used in a sentence, they are indicated by verb endings instead; for example— 'paṭhāmi' implies the same expression as 'aham paṭhāmi' (I am reading), similarly, 'paśyasi' indicates 'tvam paśyasi' (you are seeing). The declension of yuṣmad is same as that of asmad—

	1st pers.	2nd pers.	3rd pers.
Asmad—	aham	āvām	vayam
Yuṣmad—	tvam	yuvām	yūyam

The declension of bhavad goes differently in masculine and feminine genders. The application of rules is same in context with pronouns as with nouns, while working with verbs or prepositions. With pronoun bhavad, the verb ends in 3rd person. The optional short forms for asmad and yuṣmad are also practised in certain cases—

	Asmad	yuṣmad
Accus. Case—	mā nau naḥ	tvā vām vaḥ
Dat./Gene. Case—	me nau naḥ	te vām vaḥ

Certain rules are to be followed while using these short forms, they can not be used in the beginning of a sentence and before the particles like 'ca, vā, eva, ha. These short forms may be used,

1. if only one verb is used in a sentence— śālīnām te odanam dāsyāmi. (I will give you cooked rice)

2. if a vocative case precedes a qualifying adjective— hare dayālo, naḥ pāhi. (O kind Hari! protect us.)

The short form is not used immediately after the vocative case— devāsmān (not naḥ) pāhi sarvadā. (O lord, protect us always). It may be used optionally if there is no pre-mention of a thing— dhātā te/tava bhakto'sti, tasmai te namaḥ. (brahmā is thy worshipper, to thee our reverence!) Here in the second clause of the sentence, the pre- mention (anvādeśa) is already there, hence the short form is compulsorily used. Words bhavān/bhavatī are used to indicate the courteous expression, not necessarily always implying respect— atra upaviśatu bhavān. (please be seated here) or katham vā bhavān manyate. (what is your opinion?)

2. Demonstrative Pronoun— In this category, pronoun **tad** is used; its masculine and feminine forms are **saḥ** and **sā** respectively. The declension of these two is different and in neuter gender it is different only in Nominative and Accusative Case, the rest follows the masculine formation. Word **etad** means 'this' which indicates a person or a thing nearby. It has declension in all three genders, the rule follows the same as that of pronoun **tad; idam** is also used in the same meaning. Word **adas** means 'that' (an object at a distance). These pronouns may be used independently or along with nouns, they refer to; for example—

(i) *Saḥ* *āgacchati.* (independent)
He come
dem. pron. tad mas. sing. verb pres. 3rd pers. sing.

He comes/he is coming.

(ii) *Eṣa* *nṛpaḥ.*
This king
dem. pron. etad mas. sing. noun nom. case.

This is the king.

Sometimes **idam** and **etad** pronouns indicate 'here', these pronouns are generally used in first and third person and they hint at the polite behavior of the speaker; for example—

(i) *Ayam* *āgacchāmi.*
This come
dem. pron.idam mas. sing. verb pres. 1st pers. sing.

Here I am coming.

(ii)	*Iyam*	*asmi.*
	This	be
	dem. pron.idam fem. sing.	verb pres. 1st pers sing.

Here I am.

Word **tad** has several usagcs; sometimes it indicates 'same, very'; such as—

(i)	*Tadeva*	*pañcavaṭī*	*vanam.*
	That	panchavati	forest
	dem. pron. tad sing.	noun	noun (is) nom. case sing.

This is the same Panchavati forest.

(iii)	*tāni*	*indryāṇi*	*tadeva*	*nāma.*
	That	organ	that	name
	dem. pron.tad	noun neu. pl.	demos. pron.tad	noun nom. sing.

All the organs are same, the name is same.

Tad also hints at the sense of 'significance or celebrity'; for example—

sā	*ramyā*	*nagarī*	*mahān.*
that	beautiful	city	great
dem. pron. fem. sing.	adj.	noun fem.	adj.

that beautiful city!

Sometimes it is used to put stress, for example—

Soaham	*ijyāviśuddhātmā.*
That I	offering purify soul
dem. pron. tad mas. gen. 3rd pers. 1st pers. pron. sing.	adj. noun sing.

The same myself having a soul purified by offerings.

When this **tad** word is repeated, it means 'several'—

Teṣu	*teṣu*	*sthāneṣu.*
That	that	place
demons. pron.	repeat	noun loc. plu.

In various places.

3. Relative Pronoun— yat is termed as a Relative Pronoun, it has formation in all three genders; the masculine form is **yaḥ** (sing. no), the feminine is **yā**. They both have different declensions. Its form in neuter gender is **yat**, the declension of which is different only in Nominative and Accusative Case. It may follow a correlative pronoun also. When a relative pronoun is repeated, a correlative pronoun is also repeated sometimes—

1. *yasya*	*buddhir*	*balam*	*tasya.*
That	intellect	might	he
rela. pron.	noun	noun	corre.pron gen.
gen. sing.	sing.	sing.	sing. (is)

Who is intelligent, is powerful.

2. *kriyate*	*yad*	*yad*	*eśā*	*kathayati.*
Do	that	that	she	say
verb pres.	rela.	corre.	demon.	verb pres.3rd
pass.sing.	pron.sing.	pron.	Pron.	pers. sing.

I shall do whatever she tells.

Sometimes this pronoun is joined with words like **api, vā,kiñcit, kena, kāni;** the sense it implies is 'even though, whatever or whatsoever, whosoever'—

1. *Yo vā*	*ko vā*	*bhavāmyaham.*
Whosoever	repeat	be I
rela. pron.		verb pres. 1st pers.
yat sing.		pers.pron. sing.

Whosoever I may be.

2. *Vakraḥ*	*panthā*	*yadapi*	*bhavataḥ.*
Crooked	way	even though	you
adj.	noun	rela.	pers. pron.gen.
	sing.	pron.	case sing.

Even though your track is not straight.

3.

Yena	*kena*	*prakāreṇa*	*jivāmi.*
Somehow	repeat	method	live
yad relat. pron.		noun instr. case sing.	verb pres. 1st pers.sing.

Somehow I am pulling on.

4. Interrogative Pronoun— The Interrogative Pronoun in Sanskrit is used as **kim**, its masculine form is **kaḥ**, the feminine is **kā** and the neuter form is **kim** which has different declension in Nominative and Accusative case, the rest follows the masculine pattern—

(i)

Kim	*karomi*	*kva*	*gacchāmi.*
What	do	where	go
interr. pron. sing.	verb pres. 1st pers. sing.	indec.	verb pres. 1st pers. sing.

what shall I do where shall I go.

(ii)

Lobhaśced	*guṇena*	*kim.*
Greed if	merit	what
noun indec. sing.	noun instr. sing.	interr. pron. sing.

What is the use of merit if there is greed?

Word **katara** is used to indicate 'which of the two' and **katama** indicates 'which of all'. The declension of these two pronouns goes like that of **yad** in all three genders—

(i)

Katamena	*digbhāgena*	*gataḥ*	*sa jālmaḥ.*
Which	direction	go	that rogue
interr. pron.	noun instr. sing.	verb past part.	dem. noun pron. sing.

In which direction has that rogue gone?

(ii)

Devadattaḥ	*etayoḥ*	*kataraḥ.*
Devadatta	these two	which
noun	demon. pron. abla. dual	interr. pron.(is) sing.

Which of the two is Devadatta?

5. Indefinite Pronoun— Word **kim** joined with words like **cit, svit, api,** indicates the sense of indefinite pronouns and the meaning becomes 'certain or some'—

(i) *kāsvid* *avaguṇṭhanavatī* *nāri.*
Some veil woman
inde. pron. adj. fem. gen. noun sing. nomi. case. (is)

Certain veiled woman.

(ii) *Viveśa* *kaścid* *jaṭilastapovanam.*
Enter some sage forest
verb perf. past 3rd pers. inde. pron. noun nomi. sing. noun accus. sing.

Some sage entered the forest.

Sometimes word **eka** is also added to the pronoun **kim;** for example—

kasyāpyekasya *vaṇijaḥ* *sādhuḥ* *karmakaro* *gṛhe.*
Some merchant good worker house
inde. pron. geni. noun gen. case sing. adj. noun mas. nom. case sing. noun loc. sing.

(There was) an honest servant in the house of some merchant.

When **na** is joined with this pronoun, it gives the meaning 'nobody or none'; for example—

(i) *Praviśantam* *na mām* *kaścid* *apaśyat.*
Enter no I somebody see
verb pres. par. part. pers. pron. accu. sing. inde. pron. sing. imp.past 3rd pers.

Nobody saw me when I entered.

(ii) *Na*	*viśeṣo'sti*		*kaścana.*
No	special	be	some
part.	noun	verb pres. sing.	ind. pron.

There is no difference.

Words like **eka, anya, apara, itara** indicate the meaning of 'one another', referring two persons or objects—

Ekaḥ	*karoti*	*anyaḥ*	*bhunakti.*
One	do	other	suffer
ind. pron.	verb pres. 3rd pers. sing.	inde. pron.	verb pres.3rd pers. sing.

One does another suffers.

These words are also used in plural number; for example —

Maduktam		*kecid*	*anvamanyat*	*apare*
I	speech	some	approve	other
pers. pron.sing. gen.	noun	ind. pron. plu.	verb past	ind. pron. Plu.

punar	*ninirduhuḥ.*
again	condemn
part.	verb perf.past

Some approved of my speech, others, however condemned.

6. Reciprocal Pronoun— Words like **anya, itara, para** after repetition, become **anyo'nya, itaretara, paraspara**. These words indicate reciprocity; hence they are termed as Reciprocal Pronoun. These pronouns express the meaning of' each other, one another'. Mostly these pronouns are used in Accusative case, but they can be seen in other cases also; their use is always in singular number. They are used as the first members of the compound; for example—

(i)

Parasparam	*praśansanti*	*aho*	*rūpam*
Each other	admire	what	beauty
reci. pron.	verb pres. 3rd pers. plu.	part.	noun neu.

aho	*dhvaniḥ.*
what	voice
part.	noun mas. sing.

(they are) admiring each other— what a beauty what a voice!

(ii)

Te	*parasparam*	*vivadante.*
They	each other	argue
dem. pron. mas. gend. plu.	reci. pron.	verb pres. 3rd pers. plu.

They are arguing with one another.

7. Correlative Pronoun— Words like **yādṛś, tādṛś** (in the meaning of similar to),**etādṛś** (such as), **yāvat, tāvat** (so long as), **kiyat** (how much) and **iyān** (this much) are termed as Correlative Pronouns, these are declined in all genders; for example— yādṛśaḥ (mas.), yādṛśam (neu.), yādṛśi (fem.), let us have a look at the usage—

(i)

Upadeśo	*na*	*dātwavyo*	*yādṛśe tādṛśe*	*jane.*
Lecture	no	give	like that	person
noun mas. sing.	part.	verb pot. pass. part.	corr.pron.	noun loc. sing.

Lecture should not be given to any x y z person.

(ii)

Kiyad	*dure*	*sa*	*jalāśayaḥ.*
How much	distance	that	pond
corr. pron.	noun loc. sing.	dem.pron.	noun nom. sing.

how far is the pond?

Certain pronouns are also made of Personal Pronouns; for example—**tvādṛś, mādṛś, bhavādṛś.**

8. Reflexive Pronoun— Words like **sva, svakīya, ātmīya, nija** are used as Reflexive Pronouns, their meaning is ' self, ātman; for example—

(i)	*Svam*	*nāma*	*kathaya.*
	Self	name	say
	ref. pron.	noun accus. sing.	verb imp. mood 2nd pers. sing.

Tell your name.

(ii)	*Sarpastena*		*ātmanā*	*svālayam*	*nītaḥ.*
	Serpent	he	self	dwelling	carry
	noun nom.	dem.pron. inst. sing.	ref. pron. Inst.	refl.pro. noun accus. sing.	verb past pat. sing.

He himself took the serpent to his dwelling.

(iii)	*sā*	*ātmānam*	*dhikkārayati.*
	She	self	curse
	dem. pron. fem.	ref. pron. accus.	verb pres. 3rd pers. sing.

She curses herself.

Word **svayam** is an indeclinable—

sā	*svayameva*	*tatra*	*jagāma.*
She	self stress	there	go
dem. pron.	ref. pron. inde.	part.	ind. verb perf. past 3rd pers. sing.

She herself went there.

Latin word **'ipse'** is used to indicate the same sense as that of **svayam**— self.

Ātman word is always used in masculine gender and singular number, even though it refers to nouns in other genders and plural numbers—

Na *śocāmyaham* *ātmānam.*

Not	grieve	I	self
part.	verb pres.	pers. pron.	ref. pron.
	1st pers.	nom.	accus. case
	sing.		sing.

I do not grieve for myself.

9. Possessive Pronoun— Words like **madīya, tvadīya, bhavadīya, tadīya** are known as Possessive Pronoun in Sanskrit. These pronouns decline in all genders like nouns only. **Sva, svakīya, and nija** words also work as Possessive Pronouns; for example—

(i)

Bhavadīya	*sāhasena*	*aham*	*tuṣṭaḥ.*
You self	courage	I	please
Poss. pron.	noun inst.	pers. pron.	verb past
	sing.	nom. 1st pers.	par.
		sing.	

I am pleased with your courage.

(ii)

Svakīyam	*gṛham*	*gaccha.*
Self	house	go
poss. pron.	noun accus.	verb imp. mood
	sing.	2nd pers. sing.

Go to your house.

(iii)

mayā	*tvadīyā*	*duhitā*	*dṛṣṭā.*
I	you	daughter	see
pers. pron.	poss. pron.	noun	verb past
Inst. sing.	fem.		pat. sing.

I saw your daughter.

It is observed that the job of Possessive Pronouns is generally done by Personal Pronouns in Genitive case, therefore their use is less available in Sanskrit language; for example— the use of **mama sūnuḥ or sūnurme** is more common than the use of **madīyaḥ sūnuḥ**. The thin line of difference between 'my and mine or your and yours' which is found in English language, is not seen in Sanskrit.

Pronominal Adjectives— There are many pronominal

adjectival words in Sanskrit which are either derived from pronominal roots or have same pattern as pronouns. These adjectives follow the same pronominal declension. Words like **anya** (another) **itara** (other), **katara** (which of the two), **katama** (which of many), **yatara** (that of two), and **yatama** (that of many) have the same declension in all three genders as pronoun **yad.** The comparative degree of **anya** is **anyatara** (either of the two), this follows the same pronominal declension; where as **anyatara,** not being classified as a pronoun, declines like a noun ending with **a**.

There are also other words like **sarva, viśva, sama, sima**, used in the sense of 'all', which have declension like **yad**, but in neuter gender these words end in **m** in singular number of Nominative and Accusative cases. **Ubha** in the sense of 'both', takes only dual declension, but **ubhaya** in the same sense is not used in dual declension; for example—

Ubha	Mas.	Fem.	Neu.
Nominative—	ubhau	ubhe	ubhe
Accusative —	ubhau	ubhe	ubhe

ubhaya

Nominative—

Mas.		Fem.		Neu.	
Sing.	pl.	sing.	pl.	sing.	pl.
ubhayaḥ	ubhaye	ubhayī	ubhayyaḥ	ubhayam	ubhayāni

Accusative—

ubhayam	ubhayān	ubhayīm	ubhayīḥ	ubhayam	ubhayāni

Word **sama** in the meaning of 'equal', has declension of noun ending with **a**— samaḥ samau samāḥ.

Word **antara** meaning 'outer, exterior' is used as a pronoun, hence it takes declension of **sarva** but when it precedes word **pura,** it is no more a pronoun; there it declines like a noun— antarāyām purī. Words like **pūrva**, (eastern, prior), **avara** (posterior), **dakśiṇa** (southern),

uttara (northern, superior), **apara** (other), are declined like **Rāma** in Nominative plural, Ablative and Locative singular optionally—

Nominative plural, Ablative Singular, locative Singular

pūrvāḥ/pūrve, pūrvāt/pūrvasmāt, pūrve/pūrvasmin

These words are always used as pronouns when they denote relation of space, time or person with a particular thing. **Eka, dvi** are termed as numerals and they decline like **sarva** in all three genders. Eka word, when not used as a numeral, takes dual and plural also—

As a numeral

	Mas.	Fem	neu.
Nominative sing. —	ekaḥ	ekā	ekam

Not as a numeral

	Mas.	Fem.	Neu.
Nominative dual—	ekau	eke	eke
Nominative pl. —	eke	ekāḥ	ekāni

Pronominal Adverbs— In Sanskrit there are a number of pronouns, which work as Pronominal Adverbs if they are added with affixes. These pronominal words indicate time, space or direction etc.; for example—

1. yad changes to yadā (when), yathā (as), yatra (where), yataḥ (whence)
2. tad changes to tadā (then), tadānīm (at that time), tatra (there), tataḥ (thence)
3. kim changes to kadā (when), katham (how) kutra (where), kutaḥ (whence)
4. sarva changes to sarvadā (always), sadā (ever), sarvataḥ/sarvatra (everywhere)
5. idam changes to idānīm (now), ittham (thus)
6. para changes to parataḥ (further on)
7. pūrva changes to puraḥ, purastāt (before, in front)
8. uttara changes to uttarā, uttarāṇi (in the north)

9. dakśiṇa changes to dakśiṇā, daksiṇāni (to or in the south)
10. adhara changes to adhaḥ, adhastāt (down, below)
11. avara changes to avastāt, avarataḥ (behind, below)
12. apara changes to paścāt (afterwards)

There are certain conditions when pronominal words are not used as pronouns; that is when a compound word has a pronominal word as a subordinate member or when it comes in the end of an Instrumental **tatpuruṣa** or a **dvandva—** atisarvaḥ declines as tasmai atisarvāya, not sarvasmai, similarly māsapūrva declines as māsapūrvāya or māsena pūrvāya but not māsapūrvasmai. The declension of these words goes like that of a noun ending with **a** and not like **yad.**

The Pronouns ayam and asau— The paradigm of **ayam** and **asau** seems to be different from that of other pronouns. Pronoun **ayam** is formed by adding several stems. Initially it has main stems **ay/iy** and **id,** then another stem **am** is added to the first stem to form **ayam, iyam** and **idam.** We find similar forms and same stems in Avestan language also; **aem** for **ayam, iyem for iyam**. This **iyam** is used in Old Persian for both masculine and feminine genders.

The Nominative singular **asau** has the corresponding pronoun **hāu** in Avestan. In **asau** the stems seem to have been added from pronouns **sa** and **sā**. In **amum** (Accusative singular) too the stems could have been **am + u**.

VII.2

Pronoun in Manipuri

In Manipuri, pronouns are a closed class of substantive. They are declined in cases, they indicate numbers, but they do not refer to any gender. The classification of pronoun is done in the following way : 1. Personal Pronoun 2. Demonstrative Pronoun 3. Reflexive Pronoun 4. Indefinite Pronoun 5. Interrogative Pronoun 6. Reciprocal Pronoun 7. Distributive Pronoun

1. Personal Pronoun— In Manipuri Personal Pronouns are used in all three persons and numbers, which is as follows—

Person	*sing. no.*	*dual no.*	*pl. no.*
1st person	ai (I)	ibāni (we both)	aykhoy (we all)
2nd person	naṅ (you)	nabāni (you both)	nakhoy (you all)
3rd person	mahāk (he/she)	mabāni (they both)	makhoy (they all)

Pronoun in third person does not have separate words for different genders. **Mahāk** word indicates both masculine and feminine genders. Honorific words used for second person are **adom, asom or nahāk,** which are practised in formal relations. These words are used only in singular number, to indicate plural word **mayām** (many) can be used. The dual and plural numbers are formed by adding **bāni** and **khoy** suffixes to the pronoun respectively, hence forming bound words. The Personal Pronoun can be declined in Locative case by adding **ṅondā** and in Ablative case by adding **ṅondagi** in singular number; the words are—

	Locative case (sing. no.)	Ablative case (sing. no.)
1st pers.	ayṅgondā (to me)	ayṅgondagi (from me)
2nd pers.	naṅgondā (to you)	naṅgondagi (from you)
3rd pers.	maṅgondā (to him/her)	maṅgondagi (from him/her)

The Genitive marker **gi/ki** is added to Personal Pronoun and thus it forms Possessive Pronoun; such as—

	Singular	*dual*	*plural*
1st person	aigi (my)	ibānigi (of us both)	aykhoygi (of us all)
2nd person	naṅgi (your)	nabānigi (of you both)	nakhoygi (of you all)
3rd person	mahākgi (his/her)	mabānigi (of them both)	makhoygi (of them all)

2. Demonstrative Pronoun— Word **du** or **si** are used to indicate Demonstrative Pronoun; **du** indicates a remote thing or a person and **si** indicates a thing or a person near or close by. To this either the prefix of third person **ma** or nominal prefix **a** is attached, thus the pronouns are formed—

Not at a distance	at a distance
Asi (this, here)	adu (that , there)
Masi (this)	madu (that)

These words are known as determiners, they have a very specific role in the formation of Demonstrative Pronoun. Words **asi** and **adu** refer to an antecedent, but they can be used without a prefix also. They can also refer to a noun—

1. *aṅgāṅ* *du* *ojhā gi* *macā ni.*
   Child that teacher son
   noun dem. pron. noun gen. noun cop.

   That child is teacher's son.

2. *Si* *sānapot* *sofia gi ni.*
   This toy Sofia
   dem. pron. noun noun gen. cop.

This toy belongs to Sofia.

3. *kā* *si* *yāmna* *pie.*
Room this very small
noun dem. pron. adv. adj. asp.

This room is very small.

4. *aṅgāṅ* *adu* *karāy* *cakhre.*
Child that where go
noun dem. pron. ques. verb asp.

Where has that child gone?

Words **masi** and **madu** are also used in the same context, they also refer to nominal antecedent; but their indication to closeness and distance is not as significant as that of **asi** and **adu.** They generally indicate this and that respectively; for example—

1. *Masi* *aṅgāṅ* *talle* *leirik* *pāde.*
This child lazy book read not
dem. pron. noun adj. noun accu. verb neg. asp.

This child is lazy, does not study.

2. *madu* *ojhā* *phaye.*
That teacher good
dem. pron. noun adj. asp.

That teacher is good.

These demonstrative pronouns are generally used in singular number, but when in need of plural use, word makhoy is attached with the pronoun—

Singular	**Plural**
Asi (this)	asi makhoy (these)
Adu (that)	adu makhoy (those)
Masi (this)	masi makhoy (these)
Madu (that)	madu makhoy (those)

These pronouns take declension of Accusative, Locative,

Ablative and Genitive case- markers in the same way as nouns ; for example—

Accusative case-marker—

Asi bu, masi bu— such a thing
Adu bu, madu bu— that one too

Adu bu also indicates 'but also', here **bu** is not used as Accusative case- marker.

Locative case- marker—

Asi da, masi da— here
Adu da, madu da— there

Ablative case-marker—

Asi dagi, masi dagi— because of this
Adu dagi, madu dagi— because of that

Genitive case-marker—

Asi gi, masi gi— of this
Adu gi, madu gi— of that

Na used as adverbial case-marker—

Asi na, masi na— because of this
Adu na, madu na— because of that

The two pronouns having prefix **a,** also provide base for forming several pronouns—

adu asi

Adwāyda (aroud there) aswāyda (around here)
Adum (like that) asum (like this)
Aduk (that much) asuk (this much)

Some linguists have treated **asuk** and **aduk** along with words like **mayām** (many), **pumnamak** (all) as Determinative Pronoun.

3. Reflexive Pronoun— In Manipuri language root **sā** means body (literally) and self (generally) . When this root is affixed with pronominal marker— i (I) , na (you), ma (he/ she), the word becomes Reflexive Pronoun; for example—

1st person	isā (myself)
2nd person	naṣā (yourself)
3rd person	masā (himself/herself)

These pronouns may take respective antecedents optionally—

Ai	*isā*	*si*	*thabak*	*taujage.*
		Or		
	isā	*si*	*thabk*	*taujage.*
I	myself	this	work	do
pers. pron. 1st pers. sing. no.	ref. pro.	dem. pron.	noun	future polite.

I myself will do this work.

Sā root affixed with pronouns i, na, ma also indicates health, body; for example—

(naṅgi)	nasā		phabrā?
You	your	health	good
pers. pron. gen.	pers. pron.	noun	degree question.

Is your health better?

The plural of **sā** is **sen** , it is added with 2nd and 3rd person only; when with 3rd person it gives meaning for 1st person also— **aykhoy masen** (we ourselves), **makhoy masen** (they themselves) and **nakhoy nasen** (you yourselves). **Sā** joined with pronoun, always refers to its antecedent; for example—

(i)	*Rani na*	*masāgi*	*cāk*	*thoṅge.*
	Rani	herself	food	cook
	noun nom.	ref.pro. 3rd pers. sing.	noun accu.	verb past.

Rani cooked her own food.

(ii)	*Rani na*	*mahākgi*	*cāk*	*thoṅge.*
	Rani	she	food	cook
	noun nom.	ref. pron.gen.	noun accu.	verb past.

Rani cooked her food.

In the first sentence **masā** indicates reference to the subject Rani, but in the second sentence **mahākgi** indicates ambiguous meaning; it could be for Rani or someone else.

When masā pronoun is used with the causative verb, it refers to the subject or the nominative marker in the sentence—

masāgi	*phi*	*surendra na*	*raju bu*	*suhalli.*
He	cloth	Surendra	Raju	wash
ref. pron.	noun	noun nom.	noun	verb caus.
sing.gen	accu.		accu.	

Surendra gets his clothes washed by Raju.

Here, change of position of the word **masā** does not affect the meaning; the meaning remains the same as in the following sentence—

surendra na	*raju bu*	*masāgi*	*phi*	*suhalli.*
Surendra	Raju	he	cloth	wash
noun nom.	noun	ref. pron.	noun	verb
	accu.	gen. sing.	accu.	caus.

Surendra gets Raju wash his (Surendra's) clothes.

With Locative case marker **da** in the Dative sense also the position does not change the meaning—

ojhā na	*masāgi*	*leirik*	*pawan da*	*pi.*
Teacher	he	book	Pawan	give
noun	ref. pron.	noun accu.	noun loc.	verb asp.
nom.	gen.	3rd pers.		
		sing.		

Teacher gave Pawan his own book. Or

ojhā na	*pawan bu*	*masāgi*	*leirik*	*pi.*
Teacher	Pawan	he	book	give
noun nom.	noun accu.	ref. pron.	noun	verb
		3rd pers.	accu.	asp.
		sing.		

Teacher gave Pawan his (teacher's) book.

To add more emphasis on use of reflexive, suffix **mak** is added to this pronoun; **isāmak, nasāmak, masāmak.**

Ai na	*isamak*	*thabak*	*loisalle.*
I	myself	work	finish
pers. pron. sing.	ref. pron.	noun accu.	verb asp.

I finished the work all by myself.

This **sāmak** indicates singular as well as plural number.

4. Indefinite Pronoun— In Manipuri, Indefinite Pronouns are used to indicate the unidentifiable by the speaker. Two interrogative words **kanā** and **kari** with **su** suffix are generally used as Indefinite Pronouns. Pronoun **karisu** expresses an indefinite object and **kanāsu** expresses an indefinite person but they both tell the negative sense; for example—

1.

Yum da	*kanāsu*	*caṅde.*
House	some one	enter not
noun loc.	ind. pron.	verb neg. asp.

Nobody entered the house.

2.

cākhum da	*karisu*	*cānaba*	*leite.*
Kitchen	something	eatable	is not
noun loc.	ind. pron.	noun	be verb neg. asp.

There is nothing to eat in the kitchen

Besides the above said **su** word, there are other types of words also which add to Indefinite Pronouns; they are— **no, ta,gum.** Out of these word **no** is affixed to **kanā** (person) and **karambā** (thing) to tell the positive sense, where as **ta** is affixed to **ama** to form **amata** which is used with **kanā**, **karambā** and **kari** to tell the negative sense. Word **gum/kum** added with **kari** and **kanā** gives both positive and negative meaning; for example—

Use of no—

1. *Kolej da* *kanāno* *catle.*
College somebody go
noun loc. ind. pron. verb asp.

Someone went to the college.

2. *phamuṅ da* *karambano* *amā lay.*
Bed something is
noun loc. ind. pron. be verb pres.

There is something on the bed.

Use of ta—

1. *skul da* *kanāamata* *catte.*
School some one go
noun loc. ind. pron. verb neg. asp.

Not a single person went to school.

2. *Ai na* *karamba/kari amata* *phaṅde.*
I something find not
pers. pron. ind. pron. verb neg. asp.
1st pers.
sing.nom.

I did not find a single thing.

Use of gumba:— positive

1. *karigumba* *khara* *khāu da* *lay.*
Something a bit bag is
ind. pron. adj. noun loc. be verb pres.

There is something in the bag.

2. *kanāgumba* *amā* *cauki da* *phammi.*
Someone one chair sit
ind. pron. num. adj. noun loc. verb asp.

Someone is sitting on the chair.

Use of gumba:— negative

1. *kanāgumba amata* *parikhā* *pide.*

Somebody	examination	give not
ind. pron. nom.	noun accus.	verb neg. asp.

Not a single person gave the examination.

2.	*Karigumba amata*	*phamuṅ da*	*layte.*
	Something	bed	is not
	ind. pron.	noun loc.	be verb neg. pres.

There is not a single thing on the bed.

5. Interrogative Pronoun— Interrogative Pronouns are used to ask questions. In Manipuri language, words like **karī, kanā, karamba, kayā** are termed as Interrogative Pronouns. Pronoun **karī** indicates an object, **kanā** a person and **karamba** indicates both object and person. Pronoun **kayā** is used to ask number (how many) and **kayām** to indicate quantity (how much); for example—

1.	*naṅ*	*karī*	*pāmbage.*
	You	what	want/like
	pers. pron. nom.	inte. pron.	verb unr. Asp.

What do you want?

2.	*ṅgasi*	*cāk*	*kanā na*	*thoṅge.*
	Today	food	who	cook
	adv.	noun accu.	inte. pron.	verb asp.

Who cooked food today?

3.	*Ranbir*	*karamba*	*officer no?*
	Ranbir	which	officer
	noun erg.	inte. pron.	noun.

What type of an officer Ranbir is?

4.	*Si*	*chātin*	*kayā*	*pībīge?*
	This	umbrella	how much	give
	dem. pron.	noun	inte. pron.	verb polite asp.

What is the cost of this umbrella?

5.	*Yum*	*adu*	*kayām*	*chāure?*

House	that	how much	big
noun	dem. pron.	inte. pron.	verb pres.

How big is that house?

6.

Punit na	*kayāsuba*	*phurit*	*dhobi da*	*pire?*
Punit	how many	shirt	washerman	give
noun nom.	inte. pron.	noun accu.	noun dat.	verb asp.

How many shirts did Punit give to washerman?

7.

mahāk	*kayārak*	*skul*	*catte?*
He/she	how many (times)	school	go not
pers. pron.	inte. pron.	noun dat.	verb neg.
3rd pers.nom.			asp.

How many times did he/she not go to school?

All the above mentioned pronouns decline in cases like Accusative, Ablative and Locative; pronouns **kanā, karī** take Associative case also. There are other pronouns also which are used as Interrogative Pronouns in Manipuri language—

kadāyno— which

naṅ	*kadāyno*	*leirik*	*pūmmi?*
You	which	book	like
pers. pron.	inte. pron.	noun accu.	verb pres.

Which book do you like?

kadāy— where

kadāy	*catli no?*
where	go
inte. pron.	verb pres. inte.

Where are you going?

Pronoun **kadāy** declines in Ablative and Locative cases—

(i)

rajesh gi	*yum*	*kadāy da*	*lay?*
Rajesh	house	where	is
noun gen.	noun	inter. pron. loc.	be verb pres.

Where is Rajesh's house?

(ii)

Makhoy	*kadāydagī*	*lāeno?*
They	where	Come
dem. pron.	inte. pron. abl.	verb pres.

Where have they come from?

Kadom dā— where (location)

Baby	*kadom dā*	*catlī?*
Baby	where (location)	go
noun nom.	inte. pron. loc.	verb asp.

Where did the baby go?

kadāywāy— which place

kadāywāy gi	*mi no?*
which place	man
inte. pron. gen.	noun erg. pres.

Which place is that man from?

Kadawba— why

mamā na	*aṅgāṅ*	*kadawba*	*phūrīno?*
Mother	child	why	beat
noun nom.	noun accus.	inte. pron.	verb pro. asp.

Why is the mother beating the child?

karīgī— why

naṅ na	*leirik*	*rosi da*	*karīgī*	*pī?*
You	book	Rosi	why	give
pers. pron. nom.	noun accu.	noun dat.	inte. pron.	verb pres.

Why are you giving the book to Rosi?

kadawṅgāy— when

naṅ	*kadawṅgāy*	*dilli*	*laeno?*
You	when	Delhi	come
pers. pron. nom.	inte. pron.	noun loc.	verb asp.

Which day did you come to Delhi?

Pronoun **karamkāndā** also refers to time in question but it indicates more specific time (at what time)—

mahāk	*karamkāndā*	*skul*	*catle?*
He/she	what time	school	go
pers. pron.	inter. pron. loc.	loc.	verb asp.

What time does he/she go to school?

We observe that words **daw** and **dāy** are affixed with **ka** for various meanings, **daw** is also preceded by **kam** to indicate the meaning of 'how'—

kamdawrī?
How inter. pron. do (you) verb pres.

How are you doing?

There is another expression in the same meaning—

kamāy	*taurī?*
How	do
inter. pron.	verb pres.

How are you doing?

6. Reciprocal Pronoun— In Manipuri, Reciprocal Pronouns are formed by affixing **sen** to Personal Pronouns—i, na, ma; hence they are isen (1st person), nasen (2nd person) and masen (3rd person). It is invariably used in plural number; for example—

1.

makhoy	*masen*	*phunaye.*
They	one another	beat
pers. pron. nom. plu.	reci. pron.	verb asp.

They are beating one another.

2.

Nakhoy	*nasen*	*khatnaganu.*
You	each other	fight not
pers. pron. 2nd pers. plu.	rec. pron.	verb neg. imp. mood

Do not fight with each other.

3.

Aykhoy	*isen*	*nuṅgāyraga*	*lay.*
We	each other	happy	live
pers. pron. 1st pers. pl.	reci. pron.	adj.	verb pres.

We are living together happily.

7. Distributive Pronoun— Distributive Pronoun is used to express the distribution related with noun or Personal Pronoun. There seems a lot of similarity between the Distributive and Reciprocal Pronouns, hence most of the linguists have combined them both under the same head; never the less words **amamam** and **khudiṅmak** are used as Distributive Pronouns. **amamam** means 'everyone (from many people) and **khudiṅmak** means each (from limited number of people). These pronouns decline in Nominative, Ablative and Locative cases; for example—

1.

amamamna	*masā masā gi*	*kolom*	*purake.*
Everyone	themselves	pen	bring
distr. pron. nom.	ref. pron. gen.	noun accu.	verb asp.

Everyone brought their own pen.

2.

mi	*ahum na*	*khudiṅmak gi*	*chiṭṭhi*	*iri.*
Men	three	each	letter	write
noun nom.	num. distr. pron.	noun gen.	accu.	verb asp.

Each of the three men wrote letters.

Pronominal— In Tibeto- Burman languages, Pronominal is used in two ways—Verbal Pronominal and Nominal Pronominal; in Manipuri only Nominal Pronominal is in use. The rampant use of Nominal Pronominal indicates that all things are possessed by someone or the other. This Pronominal is **i** (1st person), **na** (2nd person) and **ma** (3rd person), it is used as a prefix to the noun; for example—

Relation— ināu – my younger brother/sister,

nanāu – your younger brother/ sister

Ibok — my grandmother, nabok — your grandmother

imā — my mother, namā— your mother

mamā— his/her mother

Miscellaneous— makok— his/her head,

nakok— your head

Mabuk— his/her stomach, nabuk— your stomach

Mamay— (its) tail

Na Pronominal of naṅ (2nd person) is generally avoided in relation with elders, like nace (your elder sister), napā (your father) etc., but an elder person can address the 2nd person in this way. The use of ma (3rd person) Pronominal is quite common, it does not necessarily always indicate the relation; it is ordinarily used to express a noun— mamā— mother or his/her mother, mamay— tail or its tail, mapham— place (of stay).

Conclusion

Similarity in both Languages—

1. Sanskrit and Manipuri both languages have the tradition of using Honorific Pronouns in place of 2nd person of Personal Pronoun in order to show respect, formality, honounr etc.

2. Most of the types of pronouns found in Sanskrit can also be seen in use in Manipuri language, though we do not come across the two categories of Relative and Correlative Pronouns, which are found in Sanskrit.

3. The use of Reciprocal Pronoun is available in both the languages. The Distributive Pronoun which we see much in use in Manipuri, does not find mention by Sanskrit scholars, but never the less, words like **pratyekam, ekam ekam** etc. can be seen in use in Sanskrit language and literature.

4. In Sanskrit and Manipuri all pronouns can take case-declensions.

Idam verses adu— The Demonstrative Pronouns **idam** in Sanskrit and **adu** in Manipuri are quite identical. **Idam** indicates this and **adu** indicates that. It is likely that this Manipuri word originated from Sanskrit and it was used in the same meaning , but with time, some phonological change occurred to it with a bit of different expression. Sanskrit word **asmin** of **etad** and Manipuri word **asi** also have a lot of phonetic similarity. This **asi** word too might have gone through linguistic change with time in a slightly different sense.

Indefinite Pronoun— Indefinite Pronouns in Sanskrit and Manipuri are quite similar. In Sanskrit , words like **kaścit, ko'pi, kasyāpi** or **kenasvid** used as Indefinite Pronouns, are originally Interrogatives— **kaḥ, kim** etc. In Manipuri too, Indefinite Pronouns— **kanā, karī** which are originally Interrogatives, take the suffix like **su, gum, no** etc. to form the pronouns like **karīsu, kanāsu, karambasu** etc.

Pronominal Adverbs— In Sanskrit Pronominal Adverbs are found; **yad** changes to **yadā, kim** to **kadā, sarva** to **sarvadā** etc. In Manipuri also, there are a number of Pronominal Adverbs in use— **kadāy** word affixed with **no** becomes **kadāyno** which is a pronoun, whereas **kadāy** word used alone is an adverb. **Kadaw** word joined with **ṅgāy** indicates the meaning 'where', in the same way, **aswāydā, asidā, adudā** mean 'here'.

Dual Number— It is noteworthy that Personal Pronouns in Manipuri, are used in all three numbers in the same way as they are used in Sanskrit ; singular, dual and plural. In English and in many other languages, the dual number is not used, there are only two numbers— singular and plural.

Differences—

1. In Sanskrit short forms of **asmad** and **yuṣmad** can be used optionally in Accusative, Dative and Genitive cases but in Manipuri, there are no such short forms in practice in Personal Pronouns.

2. In Demonstrative Pronoun in Manipuri, short forms **du** and **si** of **madu/adu** and **masi/asi** are found in use, this arrangement is not available in Sanskrit.

3. The Honorific Pronoun in Sanskrit, takes verb in 3rd person, but in Manipuri it does not imply any change in the person of the verb. In fact, there is only one form of verb regarding division in person, the number does not affect the verb. The suffix used with verb remains the same; no singular, no dual and no plural number.

4. In Sanskrit 3rd person in Personal Pronoun takes all three genders— masculine, feminine and neuter, but in this regard there is uniqueness in Manipuri language. Third person Personal Pronoun **mahāk** remains the same in all genders; it is left to the user to understand whether it is masculine, feminine or neuter. **Mahāk** can mean he/she/it.

VIII. 1

Derivative Verbs in Sanskrit

A derivative verb is something which is derived from another source. Derivative verbs are those which are formed generally by adding suffix to the simple verb stem. These verb derivatives come in the Secondary Category of Conjugation and they are connected with a certain modification of the original verb stem. This style is used by the speaker to serve many linguistic purposes. In many languages, including Sanskrit this style is prevalent. Derivative conjugations are common in present tense, yet they are found in use in other tenses also.

Sanskrit grammarians have acknowledged four types of derivative verbs, namely;. 1. Causative Verb 2. Desiderative Verb 3. Frequentative or intensive Verb and 4. Denominative Verb.

1. Causative Verb—

This is the most commonly used Derivative Verb. It is used when the action is being prompted by the agent; a person or a thing causes or makes another person or a thing perform the action. In other words Causative changes the root with a simple expression, to the expression 'cause to.....; for example—

1.	chātraḥ	pāṭham	paṭhati. (Simple)	
	pupil	lesson	read.	
	pupil	reads	lesson.	
2.	adhyāpakaḥ	chātram	pāṭham	pāṭhayati. (Causative)
	teacher	pupil	lesson	teach or cause read.

Teacher	makes	pupil	read the lesson.

3.	māṇavakaḥ	kumbhakāreṇa	ghaṭam	kārayati. (Causative)
	Manavak	potter	pitcher	make
	Manavak	causes the potter		make a pitcher.

In this form **'aya'** suffix is added to the root; for example— **'aya'** to root **'budh'**— **bodhaya**, to root **'gam'**— **gamaya**, to root' **paṭh'**— **pāṭhaya** etc.

Medial or initial i, u, ṛ, lṛ have the strength to **guṇa**; such as **budh** to **bodhaya** or **vid** to **vedaya**.

A final vowel has strength to Vṛddhi; such as **bhū** to **bhāvaya**, sometimes there is no strengthening, for example— **gam** to **gamaya**.

It is observed in some roots that **p** is added before '**ay**'; root **dā** changes to **dāpaya** and **sthā** to **sthāpaya**.

These causatives can be formed in all tenses and moods, suffix **'aya'** is retained in Aorist and the Benedictive Parasmaipada. The verbs can be formed in Parasmaipada, Ātmanepada and the Passive. Causative is sometimes also used to change the Intransitive verb to Transitive verb. With Intransitive verb, the conjugation takes the Accusative;

1.	*mātā*	*s'is'um*	*s'āyayati.*
	mother nom.	child accu. sing.	sleep verb caus. pers. 3rd pers. sing.

Mother makes child sleep.

2.	*raghuḥ*	*putram*	*āgarānagarm*	*gamayati.*
	Raghu nom.	son accu.	Agra city noun accu.	go cause. verb pres. 3rd pers.sing.

Raghu makes or causes son go to Agra city.

Transitive verbs may take Accusative and Instrumental both Cases—

3.

Ṛṣiṇā	*gṛham*	*tyājayati.*
(He) saint instr. sing.	home accu.	leave verb pres. 3rd pers.caus.

He causes saint leave home.

4.

saḥ	*ṛṣīn*	*karam*	*adāpayat.*
He	the holy men	tax	pay
pers. pron. nom.	accus.	accus.	verb past caus. 3rd pers. sing.

He made the holy men pay tax.

5.

Śatrūn	*svargam*	*agamayat.*
Enemies	heaven	go
accus. plu.	accus.	verb past caus. 3rd pers. sing.

He caused the enemies go to heaven (die).

6.

brahmā'pi	*tam*	*naram na*	*rañjayati.*
Brahma too	that	man not	happy
nom.	pron.	accus.	caus.

Brahma too cannot make that man happy.

7.

guruḥ	*chātrān*	*vedārtham*	*vedayati.*
Teacher	pupils	meaning of the Vedas	understand
nom.	accus.	accus.	verb pres.3rd pers. sing. caus.

Teacher makes pupils understand the meaning of the Vedas.

8.

yajyadatto	*devadattena*	*bhojanam*	*pācayati.*
Yajyadatta	Devadatta	food	cook
nom.	instr.	accus.	verb pres. 3rd pers. sing. caus.

Yajyadatta makes Devadatta cook food.

2. Desiderative Verb ——

A desiderative form indicates the wish or desire of the

agent to perform an action; or when a person or a thing is about to perform an action. The formation of the Desiderative Verb has two characteristics— (a) suffix **s** or **iṣ** is added to the root and (b) the root is reduplicated, for example—

gacchati (goes) becomes **jigamiṣati** (desires to go), **karoti** (does) becomes **cikīrṣati** (desires to do) etc. The form denoting 'about to'— **pipatiṣati phalam** means 'the fruit is about to fall'. The Desiderative form is optional, for example—

with Desiderative	without Desiderative
jigamiṣati (desires to go)	gantum icchati.
bubhūṣati (desires to be)	bhavitum icchati.

Desiderative Verbs can be formed in all Tenses and Moods, they can take 'parasmaipada' or 'ātmanepada' according to the requirement of the original root.

*The last **i** or **u** becomes lengthened before **sa**; **ji** (to conqure) becomes **jigīṣā, śru** (to serve) becomes **śuśrūsā**.

*The last **ṛ** changes to **ir** or **ur** before **sa; tṛṛ** (to cross) becomes **titīrṣā, mṛṛ** (to die) becomes **mumūrṣā.**

*Roots ending with **u ū ṛ** and **lṛ** and roots like **grah, guh** do not take **i** with **s**— verb **nu** becomes **nunūṣa** and verb **bhū** becomes **bubhūṣa**.

*The **a** of the reduplicative syllable changes to **i; paṭha** becomes **pipaṭhiṣa.**

*The ending **i u ṛ** change into **guṇa** and then to **ay/av/ar** if they are succeeded by **iṣ** in the root; **smi** (to smile) becomes **smayiṣa,** yu (to join) becomes **yiyaviṣa/ yuyūṣa, dṛ** (to respect) becomes **didariṣa.** Sometimes **ṛ** may not take **guṇa; vṛt** (to be) may become **vivartiṣa or vivṛtsa.**

*With roots having a consonant initially, **i** or **u** as penultimate and a consonant in the end except **y** or **v,** the vowel changes to **guṇa** with suffix **iṣ**; this **guṇa** is absolutely optional— dyut (to shine) may become **didyotiṣ** or **didyutiṣa.**

Examples of the Desiderative form—

1. *kurvanneveha karmāṇi jijīviṣet śatam samāḥ* (*Gītā*).

   performing here duties desire to live hundred years. (desiderative)

   While performing duties here, one should wish to live hundred years.

2. *saḥ gṛham jigamiṣati.*

   He home desire to go. (desiderative)

   He desires to go home.

3. *aham tvām praśnam pipracchiṣāmi.*

   I you question desire to ask. (desiderative).

   I desire to ask you a question.

4. *śuśrūṣasva gurūn* ....(abhijñānaśakuntalam, 4)

   Serve Imper. elders (desiderative).

   Desire to serve elders.

5. *rājā..... mumūrṣurvyādhitaḥ.* (kathāsaritsagar 29, 157)

   The king.....about to die illness (desiderative).

   The king.......is about to die due to illness.

3. Frequentative Verbs—

The use of Frequentative or Intensive Verbs occurs when an action is repeatedly or intensely done. This form is derived from any monosyllabic root, starting with a consonant, for example— **karoti** verb derived from **kṛ** root changes to **chekrīyate** or **charkarīti**, **bhavati** changes to **bobhūyate** or **bobhavīti.** Frequentative takes suffix **ya** and then it is used in ātmanepada. When it is formed without **ya,** then it takes parasmaipada. The root is reduplicated in both forms. It is better to understand these forms as ātmanepada frequentative and parasmaipada frequentative. This form may take all the tense forms like other conjugations, but it is more commonly used in the Present Tense.

*The vowel **i** or **u** of the reduplicative syllable takes **guṇa** and **a** is lengthened, for examle—

-punaḥ punaḥ atiśayena vā karoti— cekrīyate

Again again intensely or do— does intensely or again again (frequentative).

punaḥ punaḥ atiśayena vā gacchati— jāgamyate.

Again again intensely or go— goes again again (frequentative).

*If a root is ending with a nasal consonant, the nasal changes to **anusvāra** or the nasal of the concerned class, in the reduplicative syllable; **yam** changes to **yamyamyate** or **yaṁyaṁyate** (restrains immensely), **jan** changes to **janjanyate** or **jañjanyate** (produces repeatedly). When a root is having a penultimate or **ra** by **samprasāraṇa, rī** is inserted in the reduplicative syllable; **vṛt** changes to **varīvṛtyate** (happens again and again) and **pracch** changes to **parīpṛcchate** (asks again and again).

*The roots starting with joint consonants like **vya, pra, gra,** go to the original **i, u, ṛ**; in such combinations **ṛ** changes to **ar**— **ṛ** becomes **arāryate** (goes again and again), **svap** becomes **sosupyate** (sleeps deeply), **smṛ** becomes **sāsmaryate** (remembers immensely) etc.

*There are exceptions regarding roots beginning with vowels, in such cases second syllable is reduplicated; **ūrṇuñ** becomes **ūrṇonūyate** (covers immensely), **aṭ** becomes **aṭāṭyate** (goes repeatedly), **aś** becomes **aśāśyate** (eats a lot/eats repeatedly).

*The final vowel of the root, specially **dā de dhā dhe sthā gai** etc. take **ī; dā** (to give) becomes **dīya** and in intensive **dedīya**, similarly, **dhe** (absorb) changes to **dhīya** and with intensive **dedhīya.**

*Roots like **jāgṛ** (to wake up) which have two syllables, are not seen in Frequentative forms, only monosyllabic roots have Frequentative forms.

*The Frequentative of the roots like **lup** (to cut), **sad** (to sink down), **car** (to go), **jap** (to mutter prayers) indicate the meaning of reproach at the manner of doing the action; **lolupyate** implies 'he cuts awkwardly, **sāsadyate** means' he falls down badly.

4. Denominative Verb—

A Denominative Verb is formed by adding suffix to a noun- stem. This formation apparently seems to be simple, its use is found in Present Tense mostly, though it can be formed in all tenses and moods. According to Whitney, 'Denominatives are formed at every period in the history of language, from the earliest time.' (Sanskrit Grammar, Secondary Conjugation , pg.388). Sanskrit scholars have fondly used this conjugation, one can see this type of formation in Sanskrit literature often; for example—

iha loke hi dhaninām paro'pi svajanāyate, svajano'pi daridrāṇạm sarvadā durjanāyate.

(In this world strangers behave like close relatives of the wealthy people, but to the poor their own family people behave badly.)

This derivative generally implies the meaning of 'acting like, treating someone like, wishing for etc—

śyena (hawk) becomes **śyenāyate** (acts like a hawk) or **putra** (son) becomes **putrīyati** (treats like a son), **śrī** (Lakshmi) is **śrayati** (behaves like Lakshmi), **bhū** (earth) is **bhavati** (acts like earth) etc.

The usages are formed according to the implication, with different suffixes; hence they have been discussed here under four categories with different affixes attached to the nouns.

In the Expression of Wishing—

1. Use of **ya (kyac)** suffix in parasmaipada— When a wish or desire is implied, **ya** suffix is added to the nominal stem and this derivative is formed in parasmaipada.

*Final **a** or **ā** changes to **ī** before **ya**; putram ātmanaḥ icchati— putrīyati (wishes for a son).

*A nasal is dropped before converting **a, ā** to **ī** in this form; ātmanaḥ rājānam icchati— rājīyati (he/she wishes for a king).

Final **i** or **u** is lengthened— ātmanaḥ kavim icchati: kavīyati (he/she wishes for a poet).

*Final consonant does not change in this formation; ātmanaḥ samidham icchati: samidh+yati = samidhyati (he/she wishes for holy sticks) or ātmanaḥ vācam icchati: vāc+yati= vācyati (he/she wishes for words).

*Final **o** or **au** changes to **av** or **āv**; verb **go** with **ya** becomes **gavyati** (desires for cow) and **nau** with **ya** as **nāvyati** (wishes for boat).

*This **ya** suffix is also used in the meaning of 'treating someone like'; for example— putrīyati chātram (treats the student like his son) or viṣṇūyati dvijam (treats the Brahmin like Vishnu).

*Affix **ya** is also added to the nominal stems like **tapas, namas, varivas** in the expression of practising, serving, adoring respectively; tapasyati (he practises penance), namasyati devam (he adores gods), varivasyati gurūn (he serves his teachers).

*To convey the meaning of 'wishing ardently' **sa** is added to suffix **ya** with the nominal stem; madhu— madhusyati (wishes ardently for honey), for aśva— aśvasyati (longs ardently for horse).

Suffix **kāmya (kāmyac)** is also used with the nominal stem in the same expression— putrakāmyati (he she wishes for a son) or yaśaskāmyati (she wishes for fame).

In Sanskrit language, we come across with certain nominal derivatives which have been formed off nominal bases, suffix has been added to these nominals but they do not show in the formation; for example— kṛṣṇa iva ācarati = kṛṣṇati (he acts like Krishna) sva iva ācarati = svati (he behaves like self).

2. Use of **ya** off **Kyaṅ** Suffix in ātmanepada— The use of **ya** off **Kyaṅ** suffix is added to the nominal stem to convey the same meaning as in the previous context, but this conjugation takes ātmanepada— kṛṣṇa iva ācarati becomes kṛṣṇāyate (he acts like Krishna), paṇḍita iva ācarati is paṇḍitāyate (he acts like a learned person).

*Use of **ya** can also indicate the meaning of committing crime— kaṣṭam kartum utsahate= kaṣṭāyate (he prompts to commit sin)

*It is also used to indicate happiness/sorrow— sukham veśyate = sukhāyate (she is enjoying) or dukhāyate (he suffers in pain).

*It also indicates the sense of making or doing— śabdam karoti = śabdāyate (he is making sound). vairam karoti = vairāyate (he is creating enmity)

*A noun in feminine gender drops **ī** or **ā**, with **ya** suffix— kumarīva ācarati = kumārāyate (he behaves like a girl) or hariṇīva ācarati = hariṇāyate (she acts like a female deer).

*A noun does not drop **ā** or **i**, if it has **ka** for its penultimate— pācikā iva ācarati = pācikāyate not pācakāyate (she acts like a female cook).

Use of **ya** (**kyaṣ** Suffix)— Conjugated in Parasmaipada and Ātmanepada, **kyaṣ** suffix is added to the nominal bases like; **lohita**. **paṭapaṭa** etc. and the derivative becomes lohitāyate/lohitāyati (becomes red), paṭapaṭāyate/ paṭapaṭāyati (utters the sound of paṭapaṭa).

3. Use of i (ṇiṅ and ṇic) Suffixes—

Conjugated in Parasmaipada and ātmanepada— Both suffixes **ṇiṅ** and **ṇic** are added to the nominal bases; those having ṇiṅ are formed in ātmanepada and those having ṇic are formed in parasmaipada. Both the suffixes change to **aya** in the use; for example— **muṇḍa** (head) with **ṇic** (i) becomes muṇḍayati rāghavam = he shaves Raghava, **lavaṇa** (salt) with ṇic becomes lavaṇāyati vyañjanam = she mixes salt with condiments and **vastra** (cloth) with **ṇic** becomes **saṁvastrayati** = she covers with cloth. **Puccha** (tail) with **ṇiṅ** suffix and **vi pari ut** prefix, becomes utpucchayate = raises the tail, bhāṇḍa (vessel) with ṇiṅ becomes sambhāṇḍayate = he collects together the vessels.

Suffix **ṇic** is also used in the expression 'he does and he says'— ghaṭayati— ghaṭaṃ karoti ācaṣte vā = he creates pitcher and he says.

4. Use of ya (yak) Suffix— In Sanskrit there are a number of words which may be treated as verbs as well as nouns (prātipadika), by adding **ya** suffix these words become nominal derivatives; **kaṇḍū** may mean itch (noun) and to itch also, with **yak** it becomes **kaṇḍūyati/kaṇḍūyate** (he scratches), **sukha** (happiness) becomes **sukhyati** (becomes happy) and **dukha** (sorrow) becomes **dukhyati** (becomes sad). **Payas** means milk or water, with **yak** suffix it becomes **payasyati** (the cow gives milk) etc.

5. Inchoative Verbs— Inchoatives are those compounds which may be derived from any noun, by adding root **bhū** or **kṛ** in a special manner. These inchoatives can be easily sighted in Sanskrit language and literature; the examples are— **stambha** (post) becomes **stambhībhavati** (becomes post), **surabhi** (fragrance) becomes **surabhīkaroti** = (he/she makes fragrant). **Sva,** is self, it becomes **svīkaroti** (takes in one's possession) and **śithila** (loose) becomes **śithilīkaroti** (becomes loose), **kṛṣṇa** (black) becomes **kṛṣṇīkaroti** (makes black) etc.

In all these abovementioned examples, the noun takes

ī in the end before adding **bhū** or **kṛ**—

1. kṛtyayorbhinnadeśatvāt dvaidhībhavati me manaḥ. (śākuntalam3)—

   because of two separate places my mind is divided.

2. andhīkaromi bhuvanam badhikaromi (prabodhacandrodaya 11, p.42)

   I am making the world blind and deaf.

There are other common inchoatives, used in Sanskrit literature; nouns take **sāt** before being added with **kṛ** or **bhū**, for example— agnisātkaroti = it vanishes in fire or bhasmasātkaroti = he lays in ashes.

VIII.2

Derivative Verbs in Manipuri

Manipuri language is rich in connection with Derivative Verb. There is a great number of such verbs in common use in this language and a wide range of suffixes is added to the verbs to indicate various conditions, such as Mood Suffix, Negative Suffix, Intensive Suffix, Adverbial Suffix, Nominalising Suffix, Causative Suffix, Suffix indicating togetherness, reciprocal etc. In all, 25 such types of suffixes have been listed in Manipuri language, hence this language is categorised as Agglutinative Language. Below are given various verbal suffixes—

1. Suffix indicating Mood— In Manipuri language, suffix **niṅ** indicates desire or wish. This **niṅ** suffix is mostly used with dynamic verbs which are action-related, like **pā-ba** (to read), after putting **niṅ** the verb becomes **pāniṅba** (to desire to read), **thak** (drink) with **niṅ** becomes **thakniṅba** (to desire to drink). This **niṅ** suffix may also be added to stative verbs which are known as adjectives otherwise; **wāṅ** (tall) with **niṅ** becomes **wāṅniṅba** (wanting to become tall), **noy** (fat) with **niṅ** is **noyniṅba** (wishing to become fat). The examples are—

1. *ayi leirik pāniṅṅi.*

   I book read wish (Mood).

   I desire to read book.

2. *lata klas 10 gi parikhā pīniṅṅi.*

   Lata class 10 (geni) exam give wish (Mood).

   Lata wishes to give class 10 exam.

3. *aṅgāṅ masi wāṅniṅṅi.*

   Child this tall wish (Mood).

This child wishes to be tall.

4. *rādhesyām phaniṅṅi.*

Radheshyam good desire (Mood).

Radheshyam desires to become good.

This **niṅ** suffx can be used with verb in all tenses and aspects. There is a unique arrangement regarding this suffix in Manipuri, it can also be preceded by certain suffixes; such as, Causative— **han,** Directional— **thok**, Reflexive— **ja,** Reciprocal— **na**, Benefactive— **bī**, Start— **hau** etc.; for example—

Causative— babā rām bu leirik pā han niṅṅi.

Father Ram (accus.) book read cause wish.

Father wishes to make Ram read book.

Directional— imā rajen bu phī pi thok niṅṅi.

Mother Rajen (accus.) clothes give out wish.

Mother wishes to give out clothes to Rajen.

Reflective— ayi cāk lau ja niṅṅi.

I food take myself wish.

I desire to take food myself.

Reciprocal— makhoy ani phu niṅṅi.

They both beat wish each other.

They both wish to beat each other.

Benefactive— romesh cā sem bī niṅṅi.

Romesh tea make (for him/her) wish.

Romesh wishes to make tea for him/her.

Start/Auxiliary— mahāk cāk hau/khat niṅṅi.

He/she food eat start desire.

He/she desires to start eating food or to continue eating food.

However, there are instances where **niṅ** precedes suffixes like **han/ hal, hau**, for example—

1. *ayi mahāk bu cā niṅ hallī.*

   I he (accus.) eat wish cause.

   I wish to make him eat.

2. *aṅgāṅ na saṅgom thak niṅ haurī.*

   Child (nomi.) milk drink desire continue.

   Child desires to continue drinking milk.

2. (A) Reciprocative Suffix— Suffix **na** is used with verbs (dynamic) to indicate the action being done with each other, in this usage two or more persons are involved, for example—

1. *aṅgāṅ makhoy khan na re.*

   Child they fight with each other.

   Children fight with each other.

2. *mi mayām lāu na re.*

   Man many shout with each other.

   Men are shouting with each other.

(B) Suffix indicating 'Together'— There is a suffix— **min** in Manipuri which indicates 'action done together', it is succeeded by suffix— **na**, for example—

1. *mi māṅgol da pham min na re.*

   Men courtyard (Loc.) sit together.

   Men are sitting together in the courtyard.

2. *chātra leirik pā min na re.*

   Students book read together.

   Students are reading book together.

3. Suffix to denote 'Excess'— Suffix **man/mal** is used to indicate 'excess'. When the action or a thing is in the excess, this suffix is used; hence it is evident that this suffix can be used with dynamic (action) verbs as well as stative (adjective) verbs. The examples are—

1. *bhim na cąk cā mal le.*

   Bhim (nomi.) food eat excess.

   Bhim ate food in excess.

2. *ayi nuṅthin tum mal le.*

   I afternoon sleep excess.

   I slept in the afternoon in excess.

3. *masi phamuṅ lum mal le.*

   This bed heavy excess.

   This bed is very heavy.

4. Causative Suffix— A Causative suffix is used when the action is caused by someone. In a way, there are two actions involved in such situation; a preceding action and the subsequent action. Suffix **han/hal** is used for this purpose, this suffix is also used with dynamic and stative verbs; for example—

1. *ojhā na chātra bu leirik pā hal le.*

   Teacher (nomi.) student (accus.) book read cause.

   Teacher made the student read the book.

2. *mamā na aṅgāṅ tum hal le.*

   Mother (nomi.) child (accus.) sleep cause.

   Mother made child sleep.

3. *radha na phi adu ṅgāṅ hal le.*

   Radha (nomi.) cloth that red cause.

   Radha got that cloth colour red.

This suffix **han/hal** can give two different meanings also—

1. *sugriv na bāli si hal le.*

   Sugriv (nomi.) Bali die cause.

   Sugriv caused Bali death.

2. *sugriv na bāli hāt hal le.*

   Sugriv (nomi.) Bali kill cause.

   Sugriv got Bali killed.

3. *Similarly— ibok na rubi bụ saṅgom thak hal le.*

   Grandmother (nomi.) Rubi (accu.) milk drink cause.

   Grandmother made Rubi drink milk (by someone).

4. *ibok na rubi bu saṅgom pithak hal le.*

   Grandmother (nom.) Rubi (accu.) milk make drink cause.

   Grandmother made Rubi drink milk (by someone.).

5. Reflexive Suffix— Reflexive Suffix is used in Manipuri, when the action is done by oneself, the suffix for this purpose is **ca/ja**. Suffix **ca** is used after voiceless unaspirated stop like **p, t, k** and **ja** is used after vowel and voiced consonant; for example—

1. *mamā na cāk thoṅg ja re.*

   Mother (nom.) food cook by herself.

   Mother cooked food by herself.

2. *baby tārā na saṅgom thak caye.*

   Baby Tara (nom.) milk drink herself.

   Baby Tara drank milk by herself.

The use of suffix **ca/ja** followed by marker **ge/ke,** indicates polite expression—

3. *ayi si thabak tau ja ra ge.*

   I this work do myself future.

   I will do this work myself. (let me).

4. *ayi cat ca ra ge.*

   I go (polite expression).

   Let me go or I take your leave.

6. Honorific Suffix— This Honorific Suffix **pi/bi** indicates request/respect. It has same phonological conditions as

Reflexive Suffix; suffix **pī** occurs after voiceless consonants like **p, t, k** and **bī** occurs after vowels or voiced consonants. Normally this is followed by command (imperative) marker **ro, o, tu, u**, for example—

1. *dukān da khara cat pī ro.*

   shop (loc.) bit go (request).

   Please go to the shop a bit.

2. *nanāo da leirik tāk pī ro.*

   Little brother (dat.) book teach (request).

   Please help your little brother in reading book.

This usage also indicates 'Benefactive' expression—

1. *mahāk na ahal adu gi pot pū bī re.*

   He/she (nom.) elderly person that (gen.) thing bring for him.

   He/she carried the elderly person's things for him.

2. *babā na macā gi leirik lay bī re.*

   Father (nom.) child (gen.) book purchase for him.

   Father purchased book for his son/daughter.

When suffix takes marker **ge/ke**, it indicates the expression of challenge—

1. *ayi si pijā cā bī ge.*

   I this pizza eat (challenge).

   I will eat up this pizza.

2. *ayi ahiṅ da adu yum da caṅ bī ge.*

   I night (adverb of time) that house (loc.) enter (challenge).

   I will enter that house at night.

7. Suffix indicating Superiority— Suffix **hat** indicates meaning of 'forbidding, force etc. and it is used generally with verbs like **cay** (to scold or reprimand), **lāu** (shout), **nam** (supress) etc, for example——

1. *ojhā na chātra bu cay hat le.*

   Teacher (nom.) student (accu.) scold (past part.).

   Teacher scolded student.

2. *mapā na macā bu nam hatpa yāde.*

   Father (nom.) child (accu.) suppress not possible.

   Father cannot suppress child.

3. *pesā pāyba mi laytaba bu tū hatli.*

   Money having people not having (accu.) exploit.

   The rich exploit the poor.

8. Suffix for Habitual Expression— When an action is done habitually, it takes this suffix. Suffix **kan** is used after voiceless consonants; **p, t, k** and suffix **gan** is used after vowels and elsewhere. When this suffix is used for animate objects , it indicates habitual occurrence and when it is used for inanimate objects, it expresses natural process. The verbs generally used with animate beings are **cā** (eat), **thak** (drink) **sāu** (angry) **nok** (laugh) etc. The verbs generally occurred with inanimate objects are **cāk** (burn), **iṅ** (cold), **sā** (hot), **pum** (rot) etc., for example—

1. *robin choklet cā galle.*

   Robin chocolate eat habitually.

   Robin eats chocolate habitually.

2. *sarā kofi thak kalli.*

   Sara coffee drink habitually.

   Sara drinks coffee habitually.

3. *mahāk na aṅgāṅ sāu galli.*

   She/he child angry habitually.

   She/he is angry with the child habitually.

4. *inthamthā da cāk iṅgalli.*

   Winter (loc.) food cold naturally.

   Food gets cold in winter naturally.

5. *kālen da ṅgā pumgalli.*

   Summer (loc.) fish rot naturally.

   In summer fish rots naturally.

9. Suffix indicating Excess— Suffix **man/mal** indicates excessive action. It can be used with dynamic verbs and certain stative verbs also, like— **cāu** (big), **wāṅ** (tall), **lum** (heavy), **pha** (good), **yam** (much); for example—

1. *asāyuk ayi na cāk cā malle.*

   This morning I (nom.) food eat excess.

   This morning I ate food in excess.

2. *ṅgasi nabinā tum malle.*

   Today Nabina sleep excess.

   Today Nabina slept in excess.

3. *cāk yām malli, ayi cā ṅgammoy.*

   Food excess is , I eat cannot.

   Food is too much , I cannot eat.

4. *aṅgāṅ gi khāu lum malli.*

   Child (gen.) bag heavy excess.

   Child 's bag is too heavy.

10. Directional Suffix— In Manipuri there are four suffixes which are used to indicate direction; **sin** (in), **thok** (out), **kha** (up), and **tha** (down).

Suffix **Sin**— This suffix has two other allomorphs— **cin** and **jin**. The allomorph **jin** occurs with such verbs which start with aspirated sound like **h, th, ph, kh** and end with vowel or voiced sound; for example—

1. *rajiv na ceṅ cākhum da tham jin khre*

   Rajiv (nom.) rice kitchen (loc.) keep. inside (past).

   Rajiv has kept rice inside the kitchen.

2. *phamuṅ anī asi phā jin naro.*

Bed two these tighten together (imp.)

Tighten these two beds together.

The allomorph **cin** has the same verbal conditions as **jin** except that verb should have final voiceless sound— **k, p, t;** for example—

1. *lokesh, guli yā da huk cin lo.*

   Lokesh, tablet mouth (loc.) put inside (imp.).

   Lokesh, put the tablet inside your mouth.

2. *bimola na phi anī asi tāy cin le.*

   Bimola (nom.) cloth two these stitch together (past).

   Bimola stitched these two clothes together.

The allomorph **sin** is used with the verbs which end with vowel and other consonants, for example—

1. *phi mayām manuṅ pu sil lo.*

   Cloth many inside bring (imp.)

   Bring clothes inside.

2. *aṅgāṅ anī na choklet lau sil le.*

   Child two (nom.) chocolate take inside (past).

   Both children took chocolate inside.

Suffix **Thok**— Suffix **thok/dok** or **tok** is used in the meaning of 'out or up', this has the same conditions as suffix **sin**. It also indicates 'action done completely', for example—

1. *naren na pārā pā thoye.*

   Naren (nom.) lesson read out (past).

   Naren read out the lesson.

2. *shila na prema bu vārī hāy doye.*

   Shila (nom.) Prema (accu.) story tell out.

   Shila told out the story to Prema.

3. *ukhrul da lily sāt toye.*

   Ukhrul (loc.) lily blossom up (past).

   Lily has blossomed up in Ukhrul.

Suffix **Khat**— This suffix is also used as **kat/gat**. Its phonological conditions are also the same as those of **sin**, for example—

1. *sāgat le.*

   Hot become (past).

   It has become very hot.

2. *chātra tagore pā khat le.*

   Students Tagore read start up (past).

   Students have started reading Tagore.

3. *aṅgāṅ na nuṅ khun gat le.*

   Child (nom.) stone pick up (past).

   The child picked up the stone.

Suffix **Tha**— This suffix when used with verbs like **pā** (read), **ī** (write), thak (drink) etc., indicates the meaning of 'down or to continue'. It is also used as **dha**. The examples are—

1. *san mayām sorok da ceṅ tha re.*

   Cow many road (loc.) run down (past).

   Many cows ran down the road.

2. *nupī macā asi mayām leirik pā tha/dha re.*

   Woman small these book many read continue.

   These girls are continuously reading book.

11. Suffix indicating 'Aim'— In Manipuri, suffix **ra** followed by aspect marker, is used to indicate 'aim' in a sentence. It has other allomorphs also like— **la, ṅga, ma, pa**. This suffix has the mid tone, if used in the abovementioned condition, for example—

1. *nupā macā cāk cā raye.*

   Man small food eat come (past) (aim).

   The boy came and ate food.

2. *chīnu na saṅgom thak laye.*

   Cheenu (nom.) milk drink come (past) (aim).

   Cheenu came and drank milk.

When this suffix is used with unrealised aspect marker— **kani/gani**, its tone is in the low; with the condition that it is used with the same meaning (aim/goal). The examples are—

1. *samir cāk cā ra gani.*

   Samir food eat come (future) (aim).

   Samir will come and eat food.

2. *lovely tum ma gani.*

   Lovely sleep come (future) (aim).

   Lovely will come and sleep.

Suffix **ra**, if used in mid tone and with unrealised aspect marker— **gani/kani**, indicates the duration (short). The usage apparently looks the same—

1. *samir cāk cā ra gani.*

   Samir food eat (future).

   Samir will eat food shortly.

2. *lovely tum ma gani.*

   Lovely sleep (future).

   Lovely will sleep soon.

When **ra** suffix is followed by **ga**, it indicates the meaning 'after'—

1. *ayi cāk cā ra ga lāye.*

   I food eat after come.

   I came after eating food.

2. *ramā ciṭṭhi i ra ga tumme.*

Rama letter write after sleep (past).

Rama slept after writing the letter.

12. Suffix khāy— This suffix is used to indicate 'break/ tear. There are other allomorphs also like **'kāy** and **gāy'** for the same expression. Suffix **gāy** occurs with those verbs which begin with an aspirated stop like, **ph, kh, th** and which take voiced sound in the end; for example—

1. *cā da siṅ sugāy ra ga hāpo.*

Tea (loc.) ginger pound after put (imp.).

Put ginger in the tea after pounding it.

2. *chinki na leirik segāy halle.*

Chinki (nom.) book tear cause (past).

Chinki let/got her book torn.

Allomorph **kāy** occurs with the verbs having same beginning as **gāy**, but taking voiceless stop in the end like, **k, t, p**—

1. *lousi pāt da thambāl mayām sat kāy re.*

Lousi lake (loc.) lotus many blossom/break (past).

Many lotuses have blossomed in Lousi lake.

2. *rām na ū matek amā siṅjaṅ na phak kāy re.*

Ram (nom.) wood piece one axe with (ins.) break open (past).

Ram broke open the log with an axe.

3. *sinju da canā takhāy ra ga hāpe.*

Salad (loc.) gram break/pound after put (past).

Gram has been mixed in salad after pounding it.

Suffix **that/dat** and **tat** are also used for the above expression; for example—

cikthatpa— to bite

ayi na choklet piro hāy ra ga rubi na mayāy da cikthat le.

I (nom.) chocolate give say after Rubi (nom.) centre (loc.) bite (past).

When I asked for chocolate Rubi bit it in the centre.

laythatpa— twist and break

bunti na hidāk liglī gi makhum laythat le.

Bunti (nom.) medicine bottle (gen.) lid twist and break (past).

Bunti twisted and broke the cap of the medicine bottle.

soydatpa— to cut

pālak du soy dat lo.

spinach (emph.) cut/chop (imp.)

Chop the capsicum.

settatpa—

rashi na lā siṅ du settat li.

Rashi (nom.) banana leave (plu.) tear (prog.).

Rashi is tearing banana leaves into pieces.

Suffix **thek** is also in use in the same expression, it has allomorphs like **tek** and **dek** also—

cinthekpa— pull out

ramu na wā ani wāraktagi cinthek le.

Ramu (nom.) bamboo two cluster from (abl.) pull out (past).

Ramu pulled out two bamboos from the cluster.

namthekpa— to press and bend

kuldip na yot gi rod du nam thek li.

Kuldip (nom.) iron (gen.) rod (emph.) press and bend (prog.)

Kuldip is pressing and bending iron rods.

sudekpa— pound

savita na yāyṅgaṅ akaṅgba siṅ du sudek li.

Savita (nom.) turmeric dry many (emph.) pound (pres.).

Savita is pounding the dry turmeric.

phuktekpa— pull out, break

shyām na samban amanba du phuktek li.

Shyam (nom.) fencing old (emph.) pull out (prog.).

Shyam is pulling out the old fencing.

Conclusion

After studying this morphological system in Sanskrit and Manipuri language, we observe that derivative verbs have been in use in both the languages. Causative Verbs occur most commonly in Sanskrit and in Manipuri both. The use of Desiderative and Causative Verbs is found in Sanskrit language and literature very often; in Manipuri also, these two derivative verbs are commonly used. Frequentative or Intensive Verb is also in use in Sanskrit but it is less common. In Manipuri , this form is known as Excessive Verb form. This is used only to indicate the intensive nature of the action performed. We do not see the use of Frequentative type.

The use of Denominative Verb is a unique feature in Sanskrit. One can see its use in abundance in Sanskrit literature. We do not find this type of use in Manipuri, but surprisingly, one comes across a wide range of Derivative Verbs in this language. For every expression, there is a suffix added to the verb. Mutual respect prevalent in Manipuri society, is truly reflected in this language; there is a suffix for showing honour and respect and there is a suffix for showing humility. There are many suffixes in use to indicate the action like 'breaking, tearing' etc.

Bibliography

Sanskrit—

Apte Vaman Shivaram— Sanskrit Composition, Choukhamba Sanskrit series Office, Varanasi (India) 2002

Bhandarkar R.G.— First Book of Sanskrit, Light and Life Publishers New Delhi (India) 1978

–Second Book of Sanskrit, Light and Life Publishers New Delhi, (India) 1978

Burrow T.— The Sanskrit Language, Motilal Banarsidass Publishers Private Limited Delhi (India) First Indian Edition 2001

Cardona George— Indian Linguistic Studies, Motilal Banarsidass Publishers Private Limited Delhi (India) 2002

–Recent research in Pāṇinian Studies, Motilal Banarsidass Publishers Private Limited Delhi (India) 2004

Dahiya Dr. Yajanveer— Pāṇini as a Linguist: Ideas and Pattern, Eastern Book Linkers, Delhi 1995

Iyenger D. Krishna— New Model Sanskrit Grammar, The Samskrit Education Society, Madras (India) 1969

Kale M.R.— A Higher Sanskrit Grammar, Oriental Book Centre, Delhi (India) 2004

Kielhorn F.— A Grammar of Sanskrit Literature, Choukhamba Sanskrit Series Office, Varanasi, (India) 2004

Laghusiddhānta Kaumudī (Varadarāja's) 1-4 vls. –Bheemsen Shastri, 2004 Bhaimi Prakashan, Delhi-6

Macdonell Arthur A.— A Sanskrit Grammar For Students, Reprinted 2007, Motilal Banarsidass Publishers Private Limited Delhi (India)

Maurer Walter Harding— The Sanskrit Language, An Introductory Grammar and Reader, 1995, Curzon Press, St. Johnns Studios, Church Road, Richmond Surrey

TW92QA 13.

Pathak Manish Kumar— An Introduction to Sanskrit Grammar, Bharatiya Kala Prakashan, Delhi (India) 2004

Sen Sukumar— History and Pre-History of Sanskrit, Extension Lectures, Universty of Mysore 1957

Subrahmanyam Korada— Theories of Language, D.K. Printworld Pvt. Ltd. New Delhi (India) 2008

The Mahabharata— ādi parva, Vyasa Balabaksh Shodha Sansthana, Jaipur 1989

The Mahabharata— Text as constituted in its Critical Edition vol. iv, Published by The Bhandarkar Oriental Research Institute, Poona 1975

The Aṣṭādhyāyī of Pāṇini— Vasu Srisa Chandra, 2009 Motilal Banarsidass, Delhi

Vaiyākaraṇa Siddhānta Kaumudi 1-4 vls. (Bhattoji Dikshit)— Giridhar Sharma, 2005, Motilal Banarsidass Delhi-7

Whitney William Dwight— Sanskrit Grammar, Motilal Banarsidass Publishers Private Limited Delhi (India) Reprinted 2008

Williams M.Monier— A Practical Grammar of Sanskrit Language, Munshiram Manoharlal Rani Jhansi Road, New Delhi 2000

Manipuri—

Bezbarua Ranju, Goswami Priyam, Banerjee Dipankar (eds.)— North East India Interpreting the Source of Its History 2008, Indian Council of Historical Research, New Delhi.

Bhat D.N.S. & Ningomba M.S.— Manipuri Grammar, 1997, Lincom Europa, Newcastle

Chilliah, L. Shobhana— A Grammar of Meitei 1997, Berlin and New York: Mouton de Gruyter

Dolen Hidam— Structure of Manipuri (Meiteiron) Meaning, 2004, Manipuri Language Development society, Imphal Manipur

Grierson G.A.— Linguistic Survey of India Vol.iii Reprinted 1990, Low Price Publications Ashok Vihar, Phasevi, Delhi-52

–A Linguistic Survey of India VVRI Hoshiyarpur Punjab 1972

Kabui Gangmumai— History of Manipur— Pre Colonial Period, vol. 1 1991, National Publishing House, 23 Daryaganj New Delhi

Hodson T.C.— The Meitheis, First Published 1908, Last Reprinted 2009, Low Price Publications, Delhi-52

Langackar, Ronald W.— Language and its Structure, Harcourt, Brace and World, INC 1967

Leech Geoffrey— Semantics 1974 Penguin Books Ltd. Harmondsworth, Middlesex England

Madhubala P.— Manipuri Phonology, Heiran Goithong Bazar, Imphal-795008 (India) 2002

Primrose A.J.— A Manipuri Grammar Vocabulary and Phrasebook, Asian Educational Services, New Delhi (India) 1995

Sanajaoba Naorem— Manipur Past and Present, vol. ii.1991, Mittal Publications, New Delhi-59

Singh Ch. Yashawanta— Manipuri Grammar, Rajesh Publications, New Delhi-2, (India) 2000

–Tense or Aspects in Manipuri, Senri Enthological Studies 41, Eds. Yoshio Nishi, James A. Matisoff and Yasuhiko Nagano, National Museum of Enthology, Asaka, Japan 1995

–Negation in Meiteilon, Journal of Asian and African Studies, 44, 1992 Tokyo University of Foreign Studies, Tokyo

Singh L. Iboongohal and Singh N. Khelachandra (eds.)— Cheitharol Kumbaba 1989, Imphal

Singh N.Khelchandra— Manipuri Language, Status and Importance, 1975, Ningthoukhongjam Leikai Imphal, Manipur

Singh N. Saratchandra— The Case for Case in Manipuri, 2000 P.S. Publications, Manipur

Singh W.I.— The History of Manipur (An Early Period),1986, Khagempalli Panthak, Imphal Manipur

W. Pettigrew— Manipuri Grammar, 1912, Ukhrul, Imphal Manipur

W.Yumjao Singh— An Early History of Manipur, 1966, Moirang Mayum Leikai, Sagolbandh Imphal, Manipur

–General Remarks on the Maṇipuri Language Publisher, W. Gaurchandra Singh Sagolband Imphal 1968

–Archaic Manipuri, W. Gaurchandra Sigh Sagolband Moirangyum Leirak, Imphal 1983

Unpublished Thesis—

Devi M. Bidyarani— Manipuri Verbs 2002 Department of Linguistics Manipur University, Imphal

Nonegopal N.— A Meitei Grammar of Roots and Affixes, 1987 Department of Linguistics, Manipur University Imphal

Russel Nongthombam— A Contrastive Analysis of English and Manipuri Grammatical Categories, 2007 Department of Linguistics Manipur University, Imphal

Singh Khumjam Ratan Kumar— The Lai-Haraoba of Manipur (A Social, Cultural and Historical Study), 1995 Department of History School of Social Sciences, Manipur University, Imphal

Singh Moirangthem Imocha— History of the Evolution of Manipuri Script (Meitei Mayek), 2002 Department of History School of Social Sciences, Manipur University Imphal

Singh Moirangthem Ranjit— Garibnawaz And His Times (1709—1748 A.D.) 1987, Department of History University of Manipur Imphal

Dictionary—

A Sanskrit English Dictionary— M. Monier Williams, Reprinted 1981, Motilal Banarsidaas Publications Delhi

Manipuri to English Dictionary— Dr. S Imoba

Soibam Leikai, Imphal East District, Manipur (India) 2004

New World Encyclopedia— Languages of India 2007 www.newworld encyclopedia.org/entry/Languages

Pāṇinīya Dhātvanukrama Koṣa— Dr. Avanindra Kumar, Parimala Publications, Delhi 2009

Sanskrit-Hindi Kośa— V.S.Apte 2004 Chandpol Bazar Jaipur.

Appendix—I

Sanskrit Words—	
Food	
Avalehaḥ	Sauce
Odanaḥ	cooked rice
kafaghnī	Coffee
Kṛśaraḥ	Pulao
ghṛtam	Ghee
cāyam	Tea
ciputakaḥ	Flattened rice
takram	Butter milk
dadhi	Curd
navanītam	Butter
parpaṭaḥ	Pāpaḍa (snack)
piṣṭakaḥ	Biscuit
piṣṭṭānnam	Pastry
pūlikā	Poori (bread fried in oil)
miṣṭṭānnam	sweatmeat
rasagolaḥ	Rasagulla
roṭikā	Roti (bread)
lapsikā	Halua (sweat pie)
sandhitam	Pickle
samosaḥ	Samosa (snack)
sūpaḥ	Gravy
Fruits and Vegetables	
akśoṭam	Walnut
añjīram	Fig
aṅkroṭaphalam	Pistacho
amṛtafalam	Pear
āmram	Mango
āmralam	guava
eraṇḍam	Papaya
kadalīphalam	Banana
kalindam	Water melon
kājavam	Cashew

kharbūjam	Melon
jambu	Blue berry
dāḍimam	Pomegranate
drākśā	Grape
nāraṅgam	Orange
nārikelam	Coconut
maṇḍapī	Groundnut
sevam	Apple
vātādam	Almond
ārdrakam	Ginger
alābū	Gourd
ālukaḥ	Potato
kalāyaḥ	Pees
kāravellaḥ	Bitter gourd
gṛñjanam	Carrot
gojihvā	Cauliflower
palāṇḍuḥ	Onion
pālakaḥ	Spinach
pudīnaḥ	Mint
bhiṇḍakaḥ	Ladyfinger
raktāṅgaḥ	Tomato
laśunaḥ	Garlic
haritam	Cabbage

Birds and Animals

Aśvaḥ	Horse
Ajaḥ/ajā	Male/female goat
ulūkaḥ	Owl
Kapotaḥ	Pigeon
kākaḥ	Crow
kokilaḥ	Cuckoo
kukkuraḥ	Dog
gajaḥ	Elephant
caṭakaḥ	Sparrow
mayūraḥ	Peacock
mārjāraḥ	Cat
mūṣakaḥ/muṣikā	Rat
mṛgaḥ/kuraṅgaḥ	Deer
ṛkśaḥ	Beer
lomaśī	Fox
varāhaḥ/śūkaraḥ	Pig
vṛṣabhaḥ	Bull
vyāghraḥ	Tiger
śukaḥ	Parrot

sarpaḥ	Snake
Trees and Flowers	
Aśokaḥ	Jenosia
Aśvatthaḥ	Pipal (holy fig tree)
āmravṛkśaḥ	Mango tree
kokaraḥ	Wild date tree
jambīravṛkśaḥ	Lemon tree
tālaḥ	Palm tree
devadāruḥ	Pinus deodar
nimbaḥ	Neem tree (Azadirachta Indica)
betasaḥ	Bamboo
śālavṛkśaḥ	Timber tree
śiṅśapā	Shisham tree (Dalbergia Sissoo)
indīvaram	Blue lotus
kumudam	White water lily
kuvalayam	Blue water lily
campakaḥ Champā	(Michelia Campaka)
japāpuṣpam	The China Rose
navamālikā	Jasmine
puṇḍarīkam	White Lily
makarandaḥ	Filament
mālatī	Jasmine
sthalapadmam	Rose
School/College	
anusāsanam	Discipline
avakāśaḥ	Holiday (leave)
upasthitiḥ	Presence
kaṭhinī	Chalk
kalamam	Pen
krīḍākśetram	Play ground
kulapatiḥ	Vice-Chancellor
gharṣakaḥ	Rubber
tūlikā	Pencil
patrāvali	File
paṭhanam	Reading
pāṭhanam	Teaching
pañjikā	Register
punaḥpūraṇī	Refil
pustakālayaḥ	Library
pṛṣṭham	Page
prabandhakaḥ	Manager

prācāryaḥ	Principal
prājñaḥ	Intelligent
prādhyāpakaḥ	Professor
mahāvidyalayaḥ	College
māpikā	Scale
mārjakaḥ	Duster
lipikaḥ	Clerk
sañcikā	Notebook
sahapāṭhī	Peer
samayasāraṇī	Time table
śyāmaphalakaḥ	Black board
Profession	
aṅgarakśakaḥ	Body guard
abhinetā/abhinetrī	Actor/ actress
udyānapālakaḥ	Gardener
kṛṣakaḥ	Farmer
gāyakaḥ	Singer
cālakaḥ	Driver
cikitsakaḥ	Doctor
citrakāraḥ	Painter
nartakaḥ/nartakī	Dancer
nyāyādhīśaḥ	Judge
pustakavikretā	Book seller
lauhakāraḥ	Ironsmith
śākavikretā	Vegetable vendor
svarṇakāraḥ	Goldsmith
śramikaḥ	Labour
vikretā	Sales person
vaidyaḥ	Physian
Relations	
agrajaḥ/agrajā	Elder brother/sister
atithiḥ	Guest
anujaḥ/anujā	Younger brother/sister
āvuttaḥ	Brother-in-law
janakaḥ	Father
jāmātā	Son-in-law
tanayaḥ/tanayā	son/daughter
patiḥ/patnī	Husband/Wife
parivāraḥ	Family
pitāmahaḥ/ pitāmahī	grand father/grand mother (father's side)
pitṛvyaḥ	Uncle (father's brother)
putravadhū	Daughter-in-law

prapautraḥ/prapautrī	Grandson/grand daughter
bhrātṛputraḥ	Nephew
bhrātṛsutā	Neice
mātāmahaḥ/ mātāmahī	Grand father/grand mother (mother's side)
mātulaḥ	Maternal Uncle
sahodaraḥ	Sibling
śyālaḥ	Brother-in-law (wife's brother)
svasā	Sister
svasṛpatiḥ	Brother- in-law
śvaśuraḥ	Father-in-law
śvaśrūḥ	Mother-in-law

Common Use

ākāśavāṇī	Radio
ākāraḥ	Size
udyānam	Park
kāryālayaḥ	Office
kāṣṭhāsanam	Bench
kusīdam	Interest
krīḍāpratiyogitā	Match
calacitram	Movie
cayanam	Selection
cikitsālayaḥ	Hospital
chāyākṛtiḥ	Photocopy
chāyācitram	Photograph
tricakrikā	Rikshaw
daṇḍagolaḥ	Cylindar
divasaḥ	Day
durghaṭanā	Accident
dūradarśanam	Television
dūrayantrikam	Remote control
dhātrī	Nurse
dvicakrikā	cycle
nirvācanam	Election
patrikrīḍā	Badminton
paryaṅkaḥ	Sofa
pākaśālā	Kitchen
pādakandukaḥ	Football
pārapatram	Passport
puraskāraḥ	Prize
pustakādhānam	Book rack

prātaḥ	Morning
bhāgāpūrtiḥ	Ration
bhitticitram	Poster
matam	Vote
māsaḥ	Month
mūlyam	Cost
riktasthānam	Vacancy
nirṇejakaḥ	Dry cleaner
saṅketaḥ	Signal
sabhā	Meeting
sabhāgṛham	Hall/auditorium
sambandhaḥ	Connection
śataghnī	Pistol
śirastrāṇam	Helmet
śodhyapatram	Proof
hastākśaram	Signature
yantrāgāram	Factory
yaṣṭikrīḍā	Hockey
yātrāpatram	Ticket
varṣaḥ	Year
vārtāpatram	Newspaper
vāyuyānasthāṇakam	Airport

Diseases

ajīrṇam	Indigestion
atisāraḥ	Diarrhea
kāsaḥ	Cough
jvaraḥ	Fever
pakśāghātaḥ	Paralysis
pāṇḍuḥ	Jaundice
piṭikā	Boil
pratiśyāyaḥ	Cold
pralāpakajvaraḥ	pneumonia
madhumehaḥ	Diabetes
viṣamajvaraḥ	Malaria
raktacāpaḥ	Blood-pressure
rājayakśamā	Tuberculosis
vamathuḥ	Vomit
vidradhiḥ	Cancer
hṛdayāghātaḥ	Heart attack
sannipātajvaraḥ	Typhoid

Appendix—II

Manipuri Words	
Food	
uṭī	cooked cereal/vegetables mixed with baking soda
kāṅgau	Fried vegetable
khohi	Honey
cahāu	Brown rice kheer (pudding)
cāk	cooked rice
camphut	Plain boiled Vegetables
cuhi	Sugercane juice
ṅga atauba	Fish fried
ṅgā thoṅgba	Fish curry
ṅgārī	Seasoned dry fish
ṅgāren	Frozen fish curry
borā Pakoḍā	(fried snack)
havāi thoṅgba Dāl	curry (pulses)
hay thoṅgba	Fruit sweet dish
saṅgom	milk
siṅju	spicy salad
Fruits and Vegetables	
aṅgur	Grape
alu	Potato
avāthabi	Papaya
ūmorok	a type of chilli (hot variety)
kamphoy	Pomegranate
kihom	Pine-apple
kobi	Cabbage
kobi thamcetmanbi	Cauliflower
komla	Orange
khamen	Brinjal
khamen asinba	Tomato
khuṅdrum	Gourd
camprā	Lemon
canam	Garlic

tilhau	Onion
nāsapāti	Pear
nuṅ havāy	Soya bean
puṅdon	Guava
boroy	Berry
bhelandri	Ladyfinger
maṅgrā	Sweet potato
māyren	Pumpkin
morok	Chilli
laphoy	Banana
haṅgām	Mustard leaves
haynau	Mango
havāy tharak	Green pee
siṅ	Ginger
Birds and Animals	
Iroy	Buffalo
uci	Rat
ucek	Bird
ok	Pig
kay	Tiger
kwāk	Crow
khunu	Pigeon
tenawā	Parrot
noṅsā	Lion
ṅgānu	Duck
yāw	Sheep
yen	chicken
yerum	Egg
yoṅ	Monkey
vāhoṅ	Peacock
hameṅ	Goat
haudoṅ	Cat
hui	Dog
san	Cow
sagol	Horse
sawom	Bear
sāmu	Elephant
sendrāṅ	Sparrow
Insects	
kāṅ	Mosquito
kurāk	Butterfly
tin	Insect
lī	snake

hayiṅ	Fly
Relations	
Ice	Elder sister
itaymā/innamā	Brother's wife
inãu/manãu	Younger brother/sister
ine	Father's sister
inembok	Mother-in-law
indon	Aunt (mother's sister)
pābuṅ/mapā	Father
ipu/mapu	Grand father
ibok/mabok	Grandmother
imā/mamā	Mother
Words of Common Use	
upu	Box
cākhum	Kitchen
ce	Paper
ciṅ	Hill
ciṅjāw	Mountain
kā	Room
kāṅgan/kāṅkhal	Mosquito net
kālen	Summer
kāṅjay	Hockey
kaithal	Market
khudeṅ	Tray
khudop	Ring
khuji	Bangle
khonji	Anklet
turen/turel	River
thāsī	New moon
thumok	Basket
thoṅ	Door
thoṅnāu	Window
nāpī	Grass
nuṅsit	wind
phamuṅ	Bed
phi	Cloth
may	Fire
maykhu	Smoke
māy	Face
mon	Pillow
monpāk	mattress
lambi	Way
lawpham	Paddyfield

layrik	Book
lik	Chain (necklace)
ligli	Bottle
wā	Bamboo
sakyeṅ minsel	Looking glass
samcet	Comb
siṅ	Wood
sendoṅ	Profit
sendoy	Interest
hayjrāṅ	Knife
hi	Boat
yum/yumjaw	House

Diseases

anāba	Disease
apomba	Swelling
isiṅpukcatpa	Diabetes
oba	Vomit
kokcikpa	Headache
khoṅhāmba	Diaorrea
lok thuṅba	Cold
layhaw	Fever
hāgajaba	Itching
nāmma soyba	Handicap
mit tānba	Blindness